TRANSFORMATIVE SCHOOL LEADERSHIP IN INDEPENDENT SCHOOLS: FORMING CHARACTER IN MORAL ECOLOGY

TRANSFORMATIVE SCHOOL LEADERSHIP IN INDEPENDENT SCHOOLS: FORMING CHARACTER IN MORAL ECOLOGY

EDITED BY

JAMES DAVISON HUNTER

RYAN S. OLSON

FINSTOCK & TEW LYCEUM PUBLISHERS

NEW YORK, NEW YORK

ISBN 978-1-66787-550-7

CONTENTS

1

Introduction

BY JAMES DAVISON HUNTER &
RYAN S. OLSON

Every parent in America hopes to raise children who will grow to be good—to be honest, truthful, loving, dependable, and hardworking.* Americans believe that these qualities are necessary not only for a good life, but also for the democracy their kids

---

James Davison Hunter is the LaBrosse-Levinson Distinguished Professor of Religion, Culture, and Social Theory at the University of Virginia. He is also the founder and executive director of the University of Virginia's Institute for Advanced Studies in Culture, a leading interdisciplinary research center and intellectual community. The recipient of numerous literary awards, he has authored or coauthored nine books, including *Culture Wars: The Struggle to Define America* and *The Death of Character: Moral Education in an Age Without Good or Evil.*

Ryan S. Olson is the director of the Institute for Advanced Studies in Culture at the University of Virginia and a fellow in late antiquity at the Center for Hellenic Studies at Harvard University. He has also served as the program director for educational reform at The Kern Family Foundation.

* Carl Desportes Bowman, *Culture of American Families: A National Survey* (Charlottesville: Institute for Advanced Studies in Culture, University of Virginia, 2012), 81, http://iasc-culture.org/survey_archives/IASC_CAF_Survey.pdf. Parents were asked, "How important is it that each of your children be each of the following as adults?" Percentages of respondents who reported the above qualities as "absolutely essential" or "very important" were as follows: honest and truthful, 98 percent; persons of strong moral character, 95 percent; loving, 95 percent; reliable and dependable, 96 percent; and hardworking, 95 percent.

will inherit as adults.[1] Moreover, they see schools as places where good citizenship can and should be developed.*

These aspirations are anything but new.[2] However, the circumstances in which children are raised continue to change and change rapidly.

So, how should we think about the moral formation of children today? What is the path and process by which children are formed as well-integrated individuals who are caring, honest, and trustworthy—healthy human beings living virtuous and meaningful lives as civically minded and committed members of a just community?

This question has not yet been given its due. The need to address it, however, is as important as ever, even if discussions of character, social-emotional learning, citizenship, and related concepts have been discussed more frequently in education circles in recent years.

For decades now, the disproportionate effort among educators everywhere has been oriented toward the *cognitive* development of the young.† We live in a country dominated by a knowledge-based economy, after all, and the paramount interest of parents, schools, and business leaders is determined by the needs of that economy. In this light, it is hardly surprising that we see a system that encourages a chase for the credentials that both contribute to, and signify, upward mobility. Moreover, underneath this dynamic, there are noble ideals: the goal of developing children from every background who not only achieve literacy and numeracy, but excel to their full potential through a range of cognitive abilities that allow them to take their place as independent and valued members of society.

---

* Langer Research Associates, "Critical Issues in Public Education: The 2016 Phi Delta Kappa Survey, Topline Report" (Bloomington, IN: Phi Delta Kappa, 2016), 5, http://pdkpoll2015.pdkintl.org/wp-content/uploads/2016/08/PDK2016PollToplineReport.pdf. Fully 82 percent of Americans responded that it is extremely or very important for schools to "prepare students to be good citizens."

† Numerous think tanks, university departments, and nonprofit organizations exist to understand the complex range of factors that influence the *intellectual* attainment of American schoolchildren. See, for example, the education divisions of the American Enterprise Institute, the Brookings Institution, the Hoover Institution, the Urban Institute, and the Pioneer Institute; The Program on Education Policy and Governance at Harvard University; and the Department of Education Reform at the University of Arkansas.

Yet despite this understandable emphasis in education on the cognitive development of the young, there is wide recognition that developing children's mental capacities isn't enough. Human beings, after all, are not merely cerebral, but sentient; not merely rational, but feeling—and beyond the intellectual and emotional, they are social and normative beings too. If the objective is to help shape the whole child, educators would need to address these dimensions of children's lives as well.

To be sure, a considerable and consistent effort has been made to address the so-called "noncognitive" aspects of child development. By "noncognitive," scholars and educators tend to mean the *attitudes, behaviors, and strategies* that are believed also to underpin success in school and at work—capacities such as self-motivation, perseverance, and self-control, but also empathy, honesty, truthfulness, and character more broadly. And surely the instinct is a good one: For children to flourish in schools and in their future lives, it is essential that these dimensions of their lives be developed too.

As obvious as this is, there are several reasons why the "noncognitive" aspects of child development have been given short shrift. Among them is the sense that these attributes are "soft" and difficult to measure, though a number of researchers have attempted to do so.[3] These capacities also centrally involve moral issues that can be politically sensitive in a diverse society.

And there is a further reason: Moral outlooks in America today are often confused. In a 2016 survey by the Institute for Advanced Studies in Culture, a sizable majority of Americans agreed with statements that are pluralistic* and accepted diverse views about "what is good."† At the same time, a vast majority believed in an absolute standard of right and wrong and that "we

---

* James Davison Hunter and Carl Desportes Bowman, *The Vanishing Center of American Democracy: The 2016 Survey of American Political Culture, Initial Report of Findings* (Charlottesville: Institute for Advanced Studies in Culture, University of Virginia, 2016), 72. Eighty-seven percent completely or mostly agreed that "we should be more tolerant of people who adopt alternative lifestyles," and, more radically, 70 percent that "everything is beautiful; it's all a matter of how you look at it."

† Ibid. Sixty-four percent completely or mostly agree that "all views of what is good are equally valid."

would all be better off if we could live by the same basic moral guidelines."[*]

Not least, noncognitive abilities are less relevant to the individuals' and communities' "real" interests, which lie in the acquisition of marketable skills. The economic purposes of schooling have been a focus of educational systems for at least a few decades.

Layered on top of these issues is an ambivalence about what to call these attributes.[4] For one, it is peculiar, to say the least, to lump all human qualities that are not narrowly "rational" or "cognitive" into a catch-all category defined by their negation— that is, as *non*cognitive. At the same time, the very term "noncognitive" relegates the complexity of those aspects of human life and experience to a category that is subordinate, inferior, or derivative. Finally, the term "noncognitive" creates a dualism that is not only facile, but unsustainable. How, after all, can one separate the rational parts of life from the emotional and moral parts? How does anyone keep a job without a tacit commitment to truth-telling and promise-keeping? Why would anyone work for a company that is known to lie to its employees or to compensate them unfairly? More broadly still, how can one have a healthy economy without mutual trust—a trust that one isn't being cheated or deceived or taken advantage of? Even the most "rational" or calculating spheres of modern life are built upon "nonrational" foundations.

THE PSYCHOLOGISTIC ACCOUNT

The most prominent paradigm used to understand the moral formation of the young comes from academic psychology. Given psychology's concern to understand individual mental and emotional pathology and health, it would be odd for psychology not to be prominent in some ways. What is curious is that psychology basically stands alone. Even though the formation of children is a fundamental aspect of all human experience and is found in every human civilization, the perspectives of history, philosophy,

---

[*] Ibid. Given the statement that "some things are absolutely right and wrong, whether or not people can see it or recognize it," 87 percent completely or mostly agreed; the total was 82 percent for the statement that we would be better off living by the same moral guidelines.

sociology, anthropology, and religious studies have largely been absent from the discussion.

As the dominant discipline for understanding and inquiry into this puzzle, academic psychology has provided valuable insight. In recent decades, it has provided the inspiration for several accounts of moral development. For a time, it was popular to see moral development as a process by which children could "clarify" their own values. "Values clarification" didn't so much tell children what values to live by as provide them a method of self-assessment through which they could sort through competing influences in their lives to discover the values they wanted to live by. Another popular approach viewed the child's moral development as a process co-extensive with the stages of *cognitive* development. By these lights, healthy moral development involved six stages that began with individually-oriented morality, rose to socially-oriented morality, and culminated in reason-centered universal morality. Still another approach identified self-esteem and self-actualization as the highest levels of human development: Those with high self-esteem would have confidence in their own values, high regard for their own dignity, sensitivity to the feelings and needs of others, and the ability to work responsibly to solve problems. Still another version of this perspective emphasized the child's need to have positive emotions in order to flourish.

What all of these approaches had in common was the belief that the moral and character development of children were potentialities that lay emergent within the minds and emotions of every child; that the key to moral development was to call out these capacities through various techniques of self-understanding and self-improvement.

The Case of Martin Luther King Jr.

This all sounds promising, but the shortcomings of this general approach come into relief in part by how it understands moral exemplars such as Mohandas Gandhi, Jesus of Nazareth, GautamaBuddha, and Martin Luther King Jr. Though Lawrence Kohlberg's cognitive developmentalism is distinctive, his treatment of Martin Luther King is fairly typical of the broader approach. In his *Letter from a Birmingham Jail*, King wrote one may well ask, "How can you advocate breaking some laws and obeying others?" The answer lies in the fact that there are two types of laws, just and unjust. One has not only a legal but a moral responsibility to obey just laws. One has a moral responsibility to disobey unjust laws. Any law that uplifts human personality is just, any law that degrades human personality is unjust.

For Kohlberg, this kind of thinking was evidence that King personified the ideals of a "just" human being. King exemplified "stage six" moral reasoning: autonomous, conscience-oriented morality pointing toward universal principles of justice.[5]

But how did King arrive at this level of moral development? Truly, King's moral psychology was extraordinary, but by Kohlberg's account, there is no essential relationship between the content of his character and the influences of his parents, Alberta and Martin Luther King, Sr., his mentor, Dr. Benjamin Mays, the church he grew up in, his personal faith and theological training, his heritage as a southerner, his race and the legacies of racism, or his generational moment. All of the particularities that shaped him as a "stage six" moral exemplar didn't figure into the model of his formation. All of the concrete influences over many years that defined his moral vision, that fueled his moral courage, and sustained his extraordinary moral leadership in the civil rights movement were somehow incidental or, at best, peripheral to King's formation.

How can this be? As a rule, most parents are acutely aware of the influences that shape their own children's lives. As with King, children live in, and are influenced by, their particular families and communities, and the resulting configurations are almost infinitely variable. Children are further molded by a wide range of organizations—not least any schools they attend, clubs they belong to, or churches, synagogues, or mosques they worship in—and by the adults who preside within these organizations. They are shaped by their peers and by the ubiquitous influences of popular culture.

While there is much to commend in academic psychology, on its face it would seem to be limited in its ability to account for the complex processes by which children are formed morally. For generations, the field has tended to focus on the internal dynamics of how a child's character takes shape, largely disregarding the external environment that influences them. Its account of morality and the processes by which children acquire it, then, have ignored important realities that are integral to a child's moral and character development.

The reality, of course, is that the actual moral development of real children is defined by the endless particularity of the worlds they live in. To understand how these factors together influence the moral formation of children requires one to better account for that particularity.

Some scholars are recognizing this need. In civic education, recent scholarship found that "it is the norms within the adolescent's *community*, defined in this case as the high school, that matter." They matter because "norms are inculcated within collectivities, such as the family, the neighborhood, and the school."[6] Another prominent report on personalized learning emphasized the importance of community for students' persistent motivation to learn and develop, as well as the need for teachers to understand their effect on the personal formation of children within the school community, beyond their influence through instruction alone.[7] Yet another influential report from a group of psychologists repeatedly suggests that context and culture are crucial to understanding character formation, requiring a theory of culture that to date has not been available.[8]

A RICHER ACCOUNT

The Content of Their Character initiated an effort to broaden the perspective by which we understand the complexities of the moral and character formation of children. The prima facie case for the need of a broadened perspective is compelling enough. But there is social scientific evidence for this case as well.

Consider, for example, a comparison of different school types. Research suggests that nonpublic schools, and religious ones in particular, may have better success than public schools in closing the academic achievement gap and in forming civic virtues.[9] A review of the empirical literature on civic education by David Campbell indicates that private schools, particularly Catholic ones, may do a better job than public schools in inculcating citizenship behavior in such areas as civic skills, community service, political knowledge, and social tolerance, even when controlling for family income and educational levels.* Against the longstanding fears that religious schools balkanize society by producing civic separatists, a recent study of 24- to 39-year-old graduates of American Christian schools suggests that their adult participation in community is at least comparable to that of their public school peers.[10] Other scholars have noted the positive civic and academic outcomes that accompany state-subsidized "intentional" schools—often, but not necessarily, religious—in other places around the world.[11] And even though American public schools may not adopt a religious framework, when they *do* create school cultures that are more academically rigorous and morally demanding, they are more likely to foster moral values, citizenship skills, and academic achievement in their graduates.[12]

The evidence is far from conclusive, of course: Some scholars note that, in general, the differences between *schools* are more noteworthy than those between school *sectors*.[13] At the very least, until we understand the mechanisms through which these schools improve character and civic education, we can have little (or at least less) confidence in the school and sector correlations.

All of this research suggests that the sources and settings for moral and civic education matter—that the "thickness" of cultural endowments and the "density" of moral community within which those endowments find expression are significant in the formation of personal and public virtue in children.

A Broadening Perspective

To begin to broaden the perspective in more satisfying ways it is necessary to work with a different conceptual lens. We begin with a few basic definitions and we begin at the beginning.

First, morality: Morality is the realm of the good and the right; the good we, as individuals and communities, aspire to become and the right we are obligated to do, including the justice we are obligated to pursue. This is the *form* of morality. The *substance*

---

* David E. Campbell, "The Civic Side of School Choice: An Empirical Analysis of Civic Education in Public and Private Schools," *Brigham Young Law Review* 2008, no. 2 (May 2008): 487–523, https://digitalcommons.law.byu.edu/cgi/viewcontent.cgi?article=2404&context=lawreview. Note that Protestant schools were superior in three out of four measures but fell short of public school outcomes in "social tolerance."

of morality will vary according to history and cultural circumstance.* Both in form and substance, morality takes expression symbolically in its ideals, but also practically in its institutions, habits of life, and character ideals.

Character is the embodiment of a morality within a person and it, too, is a matter of form and substance. In its formal sense, character is comprised of moral discipline, moral attachment, and moral autonomy: the capacities of an individual to inhibit his or her personal appetites or interests on behalf of a greater good, to affirm and live by the ideals of a greater good, and to freely make ethical decisions for or against those goods.† Character is

---

* This is not to say that at the level of meta-ethics there are not widely shared values across time and culture. To acknowledge the importance of history and culture is not to embrace moral relativism. As discussed in James Davison Hunter's *The Death of Character*, "We need to consider again the Enlightenment commitment to create a universal and inclusive moral vocabulary capable of satisfying everyone. Its consequences, as we have seen, are not salutary for moral education and they are dubious for democracy. Thus, if one is to create greater space in our public culture for differences in moral communities to exist, it is essential to abandon the high priority we give to this commitment. To do so does not mean the sacrifice of a common public life defined by commonly held moral ideals. But instead of forcing commonality in our moral discourse at the expense of particularity, one *discovers* commonality *through* particularity. Certainly the humanist, the Jew, and the Christian who join in condemnation of racism will differ over whether humanist, Jewish, and Christian conviction provide the most trustworthy reasons for their agreement, yet each provides thick moral arguments that preserve the most important commitments of the other. We will most certainly discover other moral agreements about integrity, fairness, altruism, responsibility, respect, valor—agreements too numerous to mention. But these agreements will be found within moral diversity not in spite of it. Where disagreements remain, they can be addressed through a substantive engagement that enhances rather than undermines democracy." (Notes omitted; emphasis in the original.) James Davison Hunter, *The Death of Character: Moral Education in an Age Without Good or Evil* (New York: Basic Books, 2000), 230–31.

† This, too, draws from James Davison Hunter, *The Death of Character: Moral Education in an Age Without Good or Evil* (New York: Basic Books, 2000). Moral discipline "is the inner capacity for restraint—an ability to inhibit oneself in one's passions, desires, and habits within the boundaries of a moral order. Moral discipline, in many respects, is the capacity to say 'no'; its function, to inhibit and constrain personal appetites on behalf of a greater good. This idea of a greater good points to a second element, *moral attachment*. Character...is defined not just negatively, but positively as well. It reflects the affirmation of our commitments to a larger community, the embrace of an ideal that attracts us, draws us, animates us, inspires us. Affirmation and interdiction, the 'yes' and the 'no'—what Henri Bergson called the morality of aspiration and the morality of obligation—are merely two aspects of the same single reality. In the latter instance, it is an affirmation of commitments we have to the larger community. Finally, character

constituted by the coming together of these moral properties in ways that work through the whole person—their emotions, cognition, and habits.* But this doesn't happen in isolation from the social world. Rather, it is formed in a "conversation" between individual subjectivity, moral ideas and ideals, and the structure of social institutions. In its substantive sense, character is constituted by the enactments of the moral ideals espoused within a tradition and enacted within the institutions of particular communities. This is so whether or not that tradition is formally articulated or even acknowledged. These virtues are, more often than not, valorized in a society's social institutions and celebrated in those exemplars who practice them well. In this way, we recognize that character can find substantive expression in innumerable ways.

When talking about the moral or normative, we are talking about a phenomenon consisting of attitudes, behavior, dispositions, sensibilities, and unspoken assumptions, and its range spans both the intimate and highly personal as well as the shared and public. In certain academic circles, these are often disaggregated into a narrow understanding of "character" as a specific list of values or traits. The fact is, the individual dimensions of morality range far beyond those specific principles to a more encompassing and interwoven cluster of moral understandings, beliefs, and commitments. In the same way, the public aspects of moral formation are often disaggregated into a narrow understanding of citizenship defined by knowledge of the political system, participation in the political process, and respect for civil liberties.[14] All of these things are important, but the public dimensions reach further as a cluster of ideas and commitments relating to justice, the common good, and the ethics of our political economy.

---

implies the *moral autonomy* of the individual in his or her capacity to freely make ethical decisions. The reason, very simply, is that controlled behavior cannot be moral behavior for it removes the element of discretion and judgment. Thus, character enacts moral judgment and does so freely." (Notes omitted; emphasis in the original.) Ibid., 16.

* In this way, character is expressed through the emotions of desire, disgust, attraction, fear, and the like, and through knowledge of commitment, choices, consequences, and habits of life that form a context of individual and social practices that routinize ethical behavior.

The Social and Moral Ecology of Formation

In short, we take it as a given that personal morality and public virtue are not only psychological categories with public meaning, but ideals that are, by their very nature and constitution, social and historical. Inevitably, the moral life is every bit as institutional as it is individual; every bit as cultural as it is subjective; and every bit an inheritance of the past as it is bound by emotional, intellectual, and behavioral exigencies of the present.[15] And so it is that the formation of character and of healthy civic virtues also involves the interplay of psychological, sociological, cultural, and historical dynamics.[*]

When social institutions—whether the family, peer relationships, youth organizations, the internet, religious congregations, entertainment, or popular culture—cluster together, they form a larger ecosystem of powerful cultural influences.[†] None of these is morally neutral. Indeed, all social institutions rest upon distinctive ideals, beliefs, obligations, prohibitions, and commitments—many implicit and some explicit—and these are rooted in, and reinforced by, well-established social practices. Taken together, these form a "moral ecology."[‡]

---

[*] Fundamentally, this is a recognition that, as Joseph Davis puts it, "a conception of ourselves…as finding our bearings within, as drawing our 'purposes, goals, and life-plans' out of ourselves, is based on ignoring or denying the dialogue, both internal and in direct conversation with others, through which our identity is formed and maintained and the significance of our personal choices made meaningful." Joseph E. Davis, *Accounts of Innocence: Sexual Abuse, Trauma, and the Self* (Chicago: University of Chicago Press, 2005), 262. That "dialogue" and its attending beliefs, practices, and norms takes place within a web of institutions.

[†] The importance of this ecosystem has been described in other empirical literature. For example, communication between parents and schools makes for better student outcomes most of the time, according to Annette Lareau, *Unequal Childhoods: Class, Race, and Family Life* (Berkeley: University of California Press, 2003), 165–197. Religious participation—the involvement of children in religious congregations—has led to improvement in academic learning. Furthermore, bridging social capital across organizations in a community significantly assists a school's ability to improve students' outcomes; where institutional dynamics are negative, schools' capabilities can stagnate. Anthony S. Bryk, Penny Bender Sebring, Elaine Allensworth, Stuart Luppescu, and John Q. Easton, *Organizing Schools for Improvement: Lessons from Chicago* (Chicago: University of Chicago Press, 2010), 117, 182.

[‡] See, e.g., Allen D. Hertzke, "The Theory of Moral Ecology," *The Review of Politics* 60, no. 4 (Autumn 1998): 629–659; Jackson Lears, "Get Happy!!" *The Nation*, November 25, 2013, https://www.thenation.com/article/get-happy-2/. Lears critiques

Moral ecologies can vary by how coherent or incoherent they are, how thick or thin, how well-resourced or impoverished, how articulate or inarticulate, and the like. Character is *invariably* formed in these moral ecologies and is reflective of them. The central question is the character and quality of the moral ecology.

It is in this light that we see the significance of a school system: Schools constitute their own moral ecosystems and are sites that advance their own particular views about human life and the just society. As Charles Glenn has put it, "Formal education... presents pictures or maps of reality that reflect, unavoidably, particular choices about what is certain and what in question, what is significant and what unworthy of notice. No aspect of schooling can be truly neutral."[16] Similarly, Anthony Bryk observed that

> important messages are conveyed through schooling about the meaning of personal life and our shared world. Embedded here are fundamental beliefs about human nature and personal goodness, about how I should live as a person, and how we should live as people. Although it is commonplace to refer to this language as personal and social development, the messages conveyed are normative and, as such, *intrinsically moral* (emphasis added).*

A school's explicit or implicit moral framework and practices cannot help but influence the outlook and character of children in a variety of ways.

Schools capture our attention because they have long been viewed as a critical locus of cultivating important moral habits; for some, even more important than the family.

---

the psychological and economic happiness literatures (which have influenced character education theories and pedagogies) for their "strikingly vacuous worldview, one devoid of history, culture or political economy."

* Anthony S. Bryk, "Musings on the Moral Life of Schools," *American Journal of Education* 96, no. 2 (February 1988): 257, https://doi:10.1086/443896. If this is true of an educational institution's influence on a person, consider how influential parents and guardians may be in transmitting inherently moral "fundamental beliefs" and stances toward the "shared world." See Christian Smith and Patricia Snell, *Souls in Transition: The Religious and Spiritual Lives of Emerging Adults* (New York: Oxford University Press, 2009), 226; Markella B. Rutherford, *Adult Supervision Required: Private Freedom and Public Constraints for Parents and Children* (New Brunswick, NJ: Rutgers University Press, 2011).

THE TEN CASE STUDIES PROJECT

The chapter that follows is part of a larger initiative on the moral formation of children called the School Cultures and Student Formation Project, launched in 2013 and spearheaded by the Institute for Advanced Studies in Culture. A central component of this initiative was a series of 10 case studies designed to understand different institutional settings and how those settings provide a moral ecology within which personal and public virtue is formed within American children.* The results of that initiative were published in *The Content of Their Character: Inquiries in the Varieties of Moral Formation* (New York: Finstock & Tew, 2018). The research is exploratory, seeking to grasp qualitatively the vastly different moral worlds mediated to children.

In this project, our researchers visited schools to understand the different ways that school experiences shape the life direction and commitments of students, and to understand the diversity of school cultures and how students contribute to and are influenced by school culture. The commitments and beliefs inculcated by the school may or may not be articulated, but they are nonetheless promoted and reinforced in school settings. In this inquiry, school practices are as important as words. How a school is organized, the course structure and classroom practices, the relationship between the school and outside civic institutions— all of these matter in the moral and civic formation of the child.

We studied high schools because character and citizenship education may be taught more formally in grades nine through twelve. Citizenship may be taught in a civics or social science class; character may be incorporated in a religion or ethics class, and moral questions may be included across the curriculum, as we found in English literature classes. At the high school level, educators tend to be willing to raise moral questions for discussion, whereas at the primary-school level, an emphasis is often

---

* Joseph E. Davis adopts a similar methodological approach in an examination of biomedicine, criticizing cases where "the clinicians' clinical gaze is directed to the somatic features of disease" and is neglectful of "the complex environmental context that can affect the onset, course, therapeutic response, and outcome of illness and that typically holds the key to devising potential means of prevention." Joseph E. Davis, "Introduction: Holism against Reductionism," in *To Fix or To Heal: Patient Care, Public Health, and the Limits of Biomedicine*, ed. Joseph E. Davis and Ana Marta González (New York: New York University Press, 2016), 7.

placed on habits and rule-following without discussion or reflection. High schools also provided us an opportunity to observe a school system's end goals for its "product," the human beings they are educating.

We used the *type* of school as a proxy for different kinds of communities. The comparative method is at the heart of social science, and so school type became a means for bringing into relief some of the diversity that exists in the moral formation of the young. In all, there were 10 school types: urban public, rural public, charter public, prestigious independent, Jewish, Catholic, evangelical Protestant, Islamic, "alternative pedagogy," and home schools.* These 10 sectors were chosen in an attempt to

---

* The sectors were chosen in part based on categories used by the National Center for Education Statistics and in part based on the research team's knowledge of American schooling. The public school sector was divided by type—traditional district schools vs. charter schools—while the traditional district schools were further divided by locale: traditional urban schools, which were 24.9 percent of all noncharter public schools in 2014–2015, and traditional rural schools, which were 28.9 percent of all noncharter public schools in 2014–2015. "Table 216.30. Number and Percentage Distribution of Public Elementary and Secondary Students and Schools, by Traditional or Charter School Status and Selected Characteristics: Selected Years, 1999–2000 through 2014–15," Digest of Education Statistics, National Center for Education Statistics, 2016, https://nces.ed.gov/programs/digest/d16/tables/dt16_216.30.asp. Note that one of our six "rural" schools was considered not quite rural, but rather "town distant," by the NCES. The school self-identified as "rural," however, and its setting did not differ significantly from the strictly rural schools we studied.

The charter school sector accounted for 6.9 percent of all public schools in 2014–2015. A reported 23.2 percent of all those charter public schools were standalone high schools, and 19.7 percent were combined primary and secondary schools. Charter schools enrolled about 5.4 percent of all public school students in 2014–2015. In our study, the charter sector included high schools in urban and suburban areas.

The study's nonpublic school sectors expanded on the NCES's private school categories based on our research team's knowledge of American schooling. The NCES divides the private school sector into Catholic schools, other religious schools, and nonsectarian schools. "Table 205.20. Enrollment and Percentage Distribution of Students Enrolled in Private Elementary and Secondary Schools, by School Orientation and Grade Level: Selected Years, Fall 1995 through Fall 2013," Digest of Education Statistics, National Center for Education Statistics, 2015, https://nces.ed.gov/programs/digest/d15/tables/dt15_205.20.asp. In fall 2013, Catholic schools enrolled 38.1 percent of all private school students and 44.9 percent of private school students enrolled in grades 9–12. In our study, the category of "other religious schools" was further divided into Jewish, Islamic, and evangelical Protestant schools. "Nonsectarian" private schools were represented by some of the study's schools in two sectors: the

represent the whole American schooling landscape. While the vast majority of American children and educators are, respectively, enrolled and employed by conventional public school districts, the diversity of educational settings highlight how different schools *qua* communities relate to and or generate different ecosystems for moral and civic formation.

At the heart of this project was a talented group of scholars from different academic backgrounds. With one exception, each scholar studied a minimum of six schools in their sector, chosen through a purposive sample. In all, 57 high schools were studied. The exception, of course, was the home-schooling sector, where 35 home-school families were studied. The objective was to produce a sample of schools within each sector that reflected geographic, socioeconomic, and, in some cases, ideological or governance diversity. For example, in the Catholic sector, it was important to include a variety of schools: single-sex, coed, diocesan, religious-order, and independent. In the Jewish sector, it was important to study the ultra-Orthodox "Haredi," modern Orthodox, Conservative, and generic community schools.*

Each school was personally visited by a scholar for roughly two weeks over the course of a year and a half. This was too little time to qualify as a full-throated ethnography, but long enough to provide a portrait of a school and the students, teachers, and faculty who inhabited it every day. That portrait was constructed through classroom observation, interviews with senior administration and faculty, focus groups with students, archival research, and attendance (when possible) at school events such as all-school service days, important masses or chapel services, and the like. In addition, project scholars explored the history of the

---

prestigious independent sector, and the alternative pedagogy sector. Our tenth sector, home schools, comprises a growing area of American education. "Table 206.10. Number and Percentage of Homeschooled Students Ages 5 through 17 with a Grade Equivalent of Kindergarten through 12th Grade, by Selected Child, Parent, and Household Characteristics: 2003, 2007, and 2012," Digest of Education Statistics, National Center for Education Statistics, 2014, https:// nces.ed.gov/programs/digest/d15/tables/dt15_206.10.asp. The number of primary and secondary homeschooled students grew by 61.8 percent from 2003 to 2012, from 1,096,000 to 1,773,000. The number of homeschooled students in 2012 represented about 3.4 percent of all US students, whether in public, private, or home schools.

* Further detail about the sampling methodology can be found in particular chapters.

school sector for which they had responsibility and the particular schools in their sample. They examined the organization of each school and its curriculum; the school ethos, as well as its practices regarding moral and civic formation; the broad demographics of the school population; and the philosophical hallmarks that made a particular sector unique—e.g., how it conceived the nature of the child, the task of teaching and formation, the purpose of education, and the role of adult authority.

The full study of which the following chapter is a part thus provides a rich qualitative exploration of the varieties of school-based moral ecosystems within which children in America are formed. To our knowledge, nothing like this has ever been done before.

New Directions

The press for universal formulae for thinking about the moral development of the young continues to hold potential. That agenda, however, has long obscured the empirical richness that exists in lived experience. Moreover, it seems to us that unless one is attempting to derive universal understanding inductively from the complexity of real life, one may end up with only unfalsifiable banalities.

It is time for social science to begin to provide an account of this complexity. By doing so, there is the promise of better understanding how we think about the moral formation of children today and better supporting all those involved in the process. This initiative represents an important step in that direction.

ENDNOTES

1 James Davison Hunter and Carl Desportes Bowman, *The Politics of Character* (Charlottesville: Institute for Advanced Studies in Culture, University of Virginia, 2000), 2–3, https://s3.amazonaws.com/iasc-prod/uploads/pdf/7ba46be86c14bfb2d154.pdf.

2 Note the recurrence of these ends of education throughout Lawrence A. Cremin, *American Education: The Colonial Experience, 1607–1783,* (New York: Harper & Row, 1970); Lawrence A. Cremin, *American Education: The National Experience, 1783–1876* (New York: HarperCollins, 1980). They are also apparent in Thomas Jefferson's vision of education. Lorraine Smith Pangle and

Thomas L. Pangle, "Thomas Jefferson on the Education of Citizens and Leaders," chap.6 in *The Learning of Liberty: The Educational Ideas of the American Founders,* American Political Thought (Lawrence: University Press of Kansas, 1993), 106–24; Diane Ravitch, "Education and Democracy," in *Making Good Citizens: Education and Civil Society,* ed. Diane Ravitch and Joseph P. Viteritti (New Haven: Yale University Press, 2001), 15–29.

3 See, for example, the assessments inventoried for each "character strength" in Christopher Peterson and Martin E. P. Seligman, *Character Strengths and Virtues: A Handbook and Classification* (New York: Oxford University Press; American Psychological Association, 2004); Gema Zamarro, Albert Cheng, M. Danish Shakeel, and Collin Hitt, "Comparing and Validating Measures of Character Skills: Findings from a Nationally Representative Sample" (EDRE Working Paper 2016-08, University of Arkansas, Fayetteville, 2016, http://www.uaedreform.org/downloads/2016/05/comparing-and-validating-measures-of-character-skills-finds-from-a-nationally-representative-sample.pdf); Martin R. West, Matthew A. Kraft, Amy S. Finn, Rebecca E. Martin, Angela L. Duckworth, Christopher F. O. Gabrieli, and John D. E. Gabrieli, "Promise and Paradox: Measuring Students' Non-Cognitive Skills and the Impact of Schooling," *Educational Evaluation and Policy Analysis* 38, no. 1 (March 2016): 148–170, http://journals.sagepub.com/doi/pdf/10.3102/0162373715597298.

4 Anya Kamenetz, "Nonacademic Skills Are Key to Success. But What Should We Call Them?," *nprED, NPR.org,* May 28, 2015, accessed June 1, 2015, http://www.npr.org/sections/ed/2015/05/28/404684712/non-academic-skills-are-key-to-success-but-what-should-we-call-them; Anya Kamenetz, "What Do We Mean When We Say 'Social And Emotional Skills'?," *MindShift, KQED News,* August 14, 2017, accessed August16, 2017, https://ww2.kqed.org/mindshift/2017/08/14/what-do-we-mean-when-we-say-social-and-emotional-skills/.

5 See Lawrence Kohlberg, "Education for Justice: A Modern Statement of the Platonic View," in *Moral Education: Five Lectures,* ed. Nancy F. Sizer and Theodore R. Sizer (Cambridge, MA: Harvard University Press, 1970), pp. 68–69.

6 David E. Campbell, *Why We Vote: How Schools and Communities Shape Our Civic Life* (Princeton, NJ: Princeton University Press, 2006), 174.

7 Deborah Levitzky, Maia Merin, Emily Murphy, and Tony Klemmer, *Mapping Mastery: Building Educator Capacity for Personalized*

Learning (Providence, RI: National Academy of Advanced Teacher Education, 2017): 18–22.

8   Alexandra Beatty, *Approaches to the Development of Character: Proceedings of a Workshop* (Washington, DC: The National Academies Press, 2017), https://www.nap.edu/read/24684/chapter/1.

9   William H. Jeynes, "Religion, Intact Families, and the Achievement Gap," *Interdisciplinary Journal of Research on Religion* 3, no. 3 (2007), http://www.religjournal.com/pdf/ijrr03003. pdf; David E. Campbell, Meira Levinson, Frederick M. Hess, eds., *Making Civics Count: Citizenship Education for a New Generation* (Cambridge, MA: Harvard University Press, 2012).

10 Ray Pennings, David Sikkink, Ashley Berner, Christian Smith, Mark Berends, Julie W. Dallavis, and Sara Skiles, *Cardus Education Survey 2014: Private Schools for The Public Good* (Hamilton, ON: Cardus, 2014), 24–25, http://www.cais.ca/uploaded/ENotify_ Docs/September_2014/Cardus-Cardus_Education_Survey_2014_ Private_Schools_for_the_Public_Good.pdf.

11 Charles L. Glenn, "What the United States Can Learn from Other Countries," in *What America Can Learn from School Choice in Other Countries*, ed. David Salisbury and James Tooley (Washington, DC: Cato Institute, 2005), 79–88.

12 Karin Chenoweth, *"It's Being Done": Academic Success in Unexpected Schools* (Cambridge, MA: Harvard Education Publishing Group, 2007).

13 Andy Smarick, *The Urban School System of the Future: Applying the Principles and Lessons of Chartering* (Lanham, MD: Rowman & Littlefield Education, 2012).

14 On this particular point, see David E. Campbell, Meira Levinson, Frederick M. Hess, eds., *Making Civics Count: Citizenship Education for a New Generation* (Cambridge, MA: Harvard University Press, 2012), 1. For an elucidation of a broader perspective on citizenship, see Lorraine Smith Pangle and Thomas L. Pangle, "What the American Founders Have to Teach Us about Schooling for Democratic Citizenship," in *Rediscovering the Democratic Purposes of Education*, ed. Lorraine M. McDonnell, P. Michael Timpane, and Roger Benjamin (Lawrence: University Press of Kansas, 2000); Julie A. Reuben, "Beyond Politics: Community Civics and the Redefinition of Citizenship in the Progressive Era," *History of Education Quarterly* 37, no. 4 (Winter 1997): 399–420. For an overview of the field of character education, see Ryan S. Olson,

"Character Education," in Education, Oxford Bibliographies Online, ed. Patrick J. Schuermann (Oxford and New York: Oxford University Press, 2011), doi 10.1093/OBO/9780199756810-0052, http://www.oxfordbibliographies.com/display/id/obo-9780199756810-0052. The full text is available at http://iasculture.org/research/publications/character-education.

15 See James Davison Hunter, *The Death of Character: Moral Education in an Age Without Good or Evil* (New York: Basic Books, 2000); William A. Galston, "Political Knowledge, Political Engagement, and Civic Education," *Annual Review of Political Science* 4 (June 2001): 217–34; William Damon, *Failing Liberty 101: How We Are Leaving Young Americans Unprepared for Citizenship in a Free Society* (Stanford, CA: Hoover Institution Press, 2011); Pamela Johnston Conover and Donald D. Searing, "A Political Socialization Perspective," in *Rediscovering the Democratic Purposes of Education*, ed. Lorraine M. McDonnell, P. Michael Timpane, and Roger Benjamin (Lawrence: University Press of Kansas, 2000).

16 Charles Leslie Glenn, *The Myth of the Common School* (Oakland, CA: Institute for Contemporary Studies, 2002), 11.

2

Prestigious Independent High Schools: Between Honor and Excellence

BY KATHRYN L. WIENS

INTRODUCTION

In this study, we defined "prestigious independent schools" as private high schools that charge substantially more in tuition than surrounding nonpublic schools. The prestigious independent school sector includes a wide variety of distinctive high school structures: The schools may be religious or secular, and they may be single-sex, coed, day, or boarding schools.

The body of empirical research focused on student moral formation in prestigious independent schools is admittedly small. Still, several studies provided a basis for exploring public and

Kathryn L. Wiens is author of the book *Boys Who Achieve* and is a widely published researcher on issues of gender and learning. She received her doctorate from Boston University, and she currently serves as the director of the Schools for Applied and Innovative Learning at Delaware County Christian School.

private virtue in our research, particularly in the realms of community, tradition, and curriculum and pedagogy.

Preparatory school communities offer an atmosphere in which
excellence is expected of all students. Traditionally, in the prep
environment, each student is expected to develop "character"
through participation not only in the classroom, but in religion
and athletics as well. Arthur Powell argued that as concerns
about self-esteem arose in the 1960s, Outward Bound and other
programs based on emotional and character development shifted
prep schools toward a greater appreciation of "social virtues
such as compassion, respect, and courtesy." Prep schools go to
great lengths to establish a strong school community through
programs that teach students how to interact respectfully.[1]

Amy Gutmann has argued that private schools will tend to
inculcate views that are inherently antidemocratic.[2] In contrast,
Patrick Wolf reviewed 21 studies of such civic virtues as "political
tolerance, voluntarism, political knowledge, [and] political
participation" and found that "the effect of private schooling
[and charter schools and magnet schools] on civic values is most
often neutral or positive"—a better overall result than what was
observed for traditional public schools.[3] David Campbell, citing
evidence from studies of both private and public schools, has
suggested that students' civic engagement may be influenced
by a school's ethos, which he describes as "norms encouraged,
shared, and 'enforced' within a school community—such as
interpersonal trust and an expectation of public engagement."[4]

OUR STUDY

Our qualitative research sought to understand the sample
schools' express reasons for valuing character formation; the
ways in which the schools sought to form the character of their
students; and the tensions that made it difficult for the schools
to fully realize their mission. The six sample high schools in this
study were as follows (using aliases):[*]

---

[*] Schools and individuals who participated in the study were promised
confidentiality. Our concern for confidentiality is also the reason some descriptive
details are omitted from the bulleted list.

- **East Coast Boarding School**, a 200-year-old coed Friends school founded in the Quaker religious tradition and situated in a suburb of a major East Coast city

- **East Coast Day School**, a coed school aiming for top-tier academic rigor in an inclusive, welcoming atmosphere, situated in a suburb of a midsize East Coast city

- **Midwestern Boarding School**, a 120-year-old all-boys military school emphasizing leadership, citizenship, and global studies

- **Midwestern Day School**, a nationally respected, independent coed school known for its pioneering, inclusive, and pluralistic policies and situated in a major midwestern city

- **Southern Boys School**, a 150-year-old, internationally recognized, and highly selective all-boys school located just outside a midsize southern city

- **Southern Girls School**, an all-girls "sister school" to Southern Boys School, with a similar code of trust, honor, and citizenship[*]

Only the first of the schools—East Coast Boarding School—had a religious mission; the other schools were secular.

The administrators and faculty of the schools that participated in this study were eager to counter the conventional view that prestigious independent high schools are junior country clubs for the adolescent rich. These educators believed that their schools, rather than being elitist, reflected the best in character education.

The sample schools had differing rationales for the value they placed on moral formation. For example, Midwestern Boarding

---

[*] This sample is not large enough to be statistically representative of the prestigious independent school sector as a whole, nor was the sample randomly chosen: We constructed it to include coed, single-sex, day, boarding, and other major types of schools typical of the prestigious independent sector. This distribution increased the variety of our sample and the probability that we would not mistake moral formation elements related to, say, boarding school environments for those specific to prestigious independent schools as a group.

School had a long history of alumni who exercised great power in the public and private sectors; the school therefore felt a tremendous responsibility to instill a moral compass in its students, since they might hold similar power in the future. This concern contrasted with the view at East Coast Boarding School, which believed it was simply harnessing the "inner light and goodness" of its students so that they could promote justice around the world. The school's focus was not on the students' professional life to come, but rather on ensuring the students' values, dispositions, and decision-making were consistent with the school's Quaker worldview.

MORAL IDEALS

The highest avowed ideals at each school were variations on maintaining personal honor and showing respect for others. Personal honor was also referred to as personal integrity.

These ideals were part of the explicit academic and educational aims of the schools; indeed, based on the sample schools, the two ideals seemed almost inherent in the nature of a prestigious independent school. Although the popular assumption might be that the schools' students are entitled and selfish, the faculty arrogant, and the administration out of touch with the "real world," the culture of the schools did not appear to be elitist. In general, students at the schools seemed outwardly focused and convinced that they had a responsibility to put others before themselves. In fact, the more a school promoted individual growth, the more uniform and selfless the student body appeared to be.

Two other findings may run counter to popular perception. One was the attempt of several of the schools—East Coast Day School, Midwestern Day School, and to a lesser extent Southern Girls School—to create a neutral moral zone in the name of inclusivity. The schools' moral logic seemed to be that a student demonstrating integrity and honor implicitly respected diversity.

A second reversal of conventional expectation was each school's ethos of student service to the broader community. The schools sent a clear message that the privileges and opportunities the students received gave them a responsibility to help those less fortunate.

MORAL COHERENCE

Each of the schools we studied had a mission, a new strategic plan, or an academic or co-curricular program that directly related to moral formation. Moreover, we found tight couplings between the curriculum, the pedagogy, and the schools' guiding moral framework.

With their financial and relational capital and their independence from external governing authorities, the schools were able to galvanize their faculty and administration behind their goals extraordinarily well. Because honor was to varying degrees the most overtly emphasized moral ideal, the schools were able to construct their leadership opportunities, student culture, and curricular and co-curricular programs around this ideal.

Our school sample, in fact, may have been unintentionally skewed. The sample schools' interest in, and focus on, moral formation seemed uncommon.

Several specific factors at the sample schools seemed to contribute to moral coherence—factors that may or may not be entirely present in other prestigious independent schools. Students, interestingly, often attributed the strong culture of their schools to an admissions process that helped ensure that the students had a solid moral character. With the exception of East Coast Day School and to a lesser degree East Coast Boarding School, the schools could be very selective in the students they admitted. Similarly, students—and some teachers—at each school contended that the people who chose to attend their schools were already virtuous, and that the school's role was to reinforce the virtue or perhaps to draw it out. All of the schools' policies, expectations, and norms seemed to contribute to a unique focus on individual honor. What resulted was an uncommon culture of trust within the student body and, to a varying degree, between the adults and students on campus.

Parents, moreover, were expected to be a part of the school community. Each of the day schools we studied had incredibly robust parent volunteer networks. The parents understood what is referred to as "the dance" at independent schools—the expectation that parents will give of their time and treasure in addition to paying tuition. The expectations placed on families all but required a sole focus on school commitments. A program that touched every part of a student's life—even family life—helped these schools create a coherent culture and a dedication to that culture.

Indeed, at each of the sample schools, we observed a strong commitment to the students outside the classroom. As we spoke with top-level administrators, we realized that these schools, boarding and day schools alike, sought students and families who were comfortable with students' dedicating all but a few waking hours a week to their school responsibilities. In many ways, these schools seemed to know that in order for their missions to be realized, they had to engage the students in many different venues and many different ways.

Hence, the extracurricular programs at these schools were sophisticated and diverse; students had many points of contact outside the classroom with adults who shared the school's vision of a life well lived. While some of the extracurricular programs were widely viewed as résumé-builders, the students and parents still expected personal attention to extend beyond class hours. As we talked to teachers about moral formation in a focus group at Southern Boys School, one teacher, a 40-year veteran, smiled and said, "Oh...the classroom is just the beginning."

To varying degrees, we saw this excitement about investing in the lives of students outside of the classroom on every campus we visited. The teachers in these schools believed they had an important job to do as they worked with some of the most talented and privileged students in the country.

The presence of such teachers is no surprise. The vast majority of schools in the prestigious independent sector have uncommon latitude in creating their curricula and enviable resources to support their programs. Because of their financial strength, these schools could provide rich professional development, create administrative positions for seeing through new initiatives, and hire remarkable teachers to implement the vision of the school through the curriculum. Real attention was paid to choices in policy and in academic and co-curricular programs.

Thus, we found passionate teachers who pursued positions at a school because of its mission, or who were recruited specifically to fill a role that met the school's mission. These teachers were granted tremendous autonomy in their classrooms, but because of the unified purpose so clear in each school, they varied very little, we found, in their beliefs and practices. Ultimately, as a teacher at Midwestern Day School observed, "When it comes down to it, nothing gets in the way of us achieving our mission. The talent of our students, the resources we have—if we can't achieve our mission, it is nobody's fault but our own."

MORAL TENSIONS

These observations should not be taken to imply that the schools were uniformly successful in delivering a moral message. There was, for instance, some disparity between the priority the schools placed on moral formation and the primary reasons parents chose the schools. Although each of the schools was critically aware of the need to cultivate character in its students, the parents—with the exception of those at the East Coast Boarding School—seemed to be more concerned with elite academic and professional achievement. These parents almost appeared to view the development of character as a nice accessory to the other benefits of a prestigious education.

This disconnect was often sensed by the students. While all of the sample schools incorporated moral pedagogy into the students' daily life, the extent to which this emphasis was recognized or appreciated by the students at each school varied greatly. Students' skepticism may be due not just to parental attitudes, but also to the conflict between the schools' explicit mission of forming moral citizens and their implicit mission as prestigious independent schools—an exceptional college preparatory education.

Hence, we observed the greatest moral incoherence in discussions with or about students. Within each school, there was a subset of students who were receiving conflicting messages from home and were even sensing incoherence in the school's messages. Except at East Coast Boarding School and East Coast Day School, a majority of the students interviewed at each school suggested that their school did not ultimately care what kind of person they became. Instead, they felt the school was most concerned about their academic achievement and where they went to college.

This dichotomy between the schools' explicit and implicit missions was also evident in the way faculty perceived their role in their students' moral formation. At those schools where students perceived academics as primary, the faculty tended also to see student academics as teachers' primary responsibility. Further, many faculty viewed the influence of the parents as a limitation on students' moral formation, perceiving the parents' chief priority to be a prestigious, top-tier education. The faculty generally regretted this dynamic, except at Southern Boys School, where teachers and parents were more united behind the primacy of academics, and at East Coast Boarding School, where teachers and parents were more united behind the primacy of sound moral character.

PRIVATE VIRTUE

At the schools we studied, it was clear that the spheres of private and public virtue were intimately linked. Most of these schools displayed a varying but significant fidelity to the idea that developing one's own character was directly related to one's ability to help others and address systemic poverty and injustice.

What, then, constituted personal character? The answer was partly influenced by the very nature of this school sector. Although the mission statements of the prestigious independent schools we studied did not refer to students who were high achievers and hard workers, the implicit message students received from home and school was that their academic achievement and matriculation to an elite college—not just any college—were paramount.[*] Perhaps for the students and administrators in these schools, the need for academic excellence was obviously inherent in the schools' program, or perhaps administrators felt the need to smooth the edges of a historical perception of their schools as rigid, exclusive clubs for those who consider themselves elite. Regardless, in a competitive market for gifted students from wealthy families, the schools and their boards knew the stakes were high in producing exceptional test scores and a long list of acceptances to the best universities.

---

[*] This message was considerably weaker at East Coast Boarding School. The parents there were still inclined to elevate academics over moral formation, but the students appeared to be even more strongly influenced by the school and its commitment to cultivating personal moral virtue.

In turn, prestigious independent schools have long capitalized on the desire of parents to have their children receive superior, challenging, and personally beneficial academic training. As one teacher at Southern Girls School cynically lamented, "You know, I don't think parents are spending $23,000 a year to instill a sense of wonder. It's about getting into a good school." Therefore, with the exception of East Coast Boarding School, it was clear that the mark of a virtuous student was his or her achievement at the school and ability to "make it" through the intense pressures of what were, at times, unrealistic demands.

And the demands placed upon students at the sample schools *were* intense. Most schools required students to participate in at least two seasons of sports while withstanding an elite academic experience that often rewarded students with four or five hours of homework per night. Each of the schools also placed a heavy emphasis on student service and leadership, demanding yet more time. The schools expected students to fully immerse themselves in the schools' cultures of excellence.

Yet as noted earlier, that culture of excellence demanded another private virtue, too. Teachers, students, and administrators on the campuses we studied made it clear that the schools had all elevated the ideal of personal honor in ways that may be unique to this sector. With clear mission statements or credos, most of which included honor as the highest ideal of character, the schools were able to architect policies and practices that helped students experience the school's definition of honor and practice living honorably. A senior student leader at Southern Girls School commented on her experience at the school with this reflection:

> The honor code is such a heavy part of what we do here; it is emphasized so much. We have to be super honorable. We, like, sign the honor code at the beginning of school. After every quiz or test, we, like, sign the code. They are super strict about honor here, and we are held to a way higher standard than kids in other schools.

Indeed, as we spoke to people and observed campus life, we never used the word "honor" in our questions. Nevertheless, the term came up with surprising consistency in these conversations and in the school documents we analyzed. While students and faculty were unsure about how long these honorable behaviors persisted after students graduated, there was clear agreement on each campus about the behaviors that were acceptable and unacceptable within the unique school community.

Without exception, each of the schools dedicated substantial financial and intellectual resources, as well as perhaps the most valuable resource, time, into developing strength of character within their students. We observed some schools in which this dedication was intentionally integrated deep into the pedagogy of the teachers and into the written curriculum; other schools took a more formal extracurricular or even an informal organic relational approach to achieving the full vision of education as mind, spirit, and body.

Given the well-defined private virtues of success and personal honor in their academic lives, however, students often perceived a palpable tension between academic achievement and virtuous living. As a senior at Southern Boys School noted, "Sometimes we are forced to be ungentlemanly to achieve the neurotic level of success the school expects."

Students often spoke to us about the frequency with which academic achievement and personal honor were at odds. At Midwestern Boarding School, Southern Boys School, and Midwestern Day School, it was clear that students often calculated the cost of sacrificing their honor as lower than the high cost of earning a bad grade. In negotiating these zones of competing virtues, many students reinforced their initial perception that the academic imperative superseded their personal honor.

The tension between the two private virtues seemed largely linked to the degree to which schools adopted the traditional markers of academic achievement, such as AP scores, SAT scores, and Tier-1 college admission. For instance, at Midwestern Day School, Midwestern Boarding School, Southern Girls School, and Southern Boys School, AP courses were centrally important and sometimes viewed as at odds with the development of virtue. The teachers likewise felt the pressure of those high stakes and often expressed frustration at the emphasis on what they believed were actually poor markers of a quality education.

In contrast, East Coast Boarding School and to a lesser degree East Coast Day School chose to minimize the emphasis placed on the traditional "prep school" markers of excellence, instead committing to a curriculum, pedagogy, and even counseling that reflected their missions over the students' résumés. Particularly at East Coast Boarding School, the students seemed not to experience a conflict between academic achievement and personal honor, even though East Coast Boarding School provided a challenging top-tier education and expected students to work hard and excel in the classroom.

The degree to which the students embraced their school's ideals was also quite different on each campus. Students were often compliant in observing the moral norms of the school, but this compliance did not necessarily equate to an honest commitment to the ideals. That commitment appeared to vary with the schools' different definitions of honor. Students seemed less likely to genuinely embrace their school's ideals at East Coast Day School and Southern Girls School, where honor was defined primarily as being true to oneself. In contrast, students seemed more likely to genuinely embrace their school's ideals at Midwestern Boarding School, East Coast Boarding School, and to a lesser extent at Midwestern Day School—places where honor was defined primarily as respecting one another. The first set of schools tended to stress the virtue of academic success, while the latter group tended to stress the virtue of social justice.

We will add one final note on honor. As previously discussed, the intense desire of families to be a part of the school community allowed a generous allocation of authority to rest with the school, and therefore most parents seemed supportive of their school's efforts to shape the honor of their children. The students, in turn, were typically quite respectful of the policies the school established.

This generalization did not hold at Southern Girls School, however. At this school, there was a clear conflict between the school's desire to shape students' virtue and the parents' general belief that the school should avoid moral formation of students altogether. The students, in general, grudgingly accepted the school's policies regarding school behavior, but did not believe in the school's system of values.

Despite what this tension at Southern Girls School might suggest, the schools' emphasis on honor did not mean the schools passed judgment on every aspect of the students' lives. We found the value of pluralism to be prominent at each school we visited, and most of the schools' policies and curriculum decisions were aligned behind the goal of promoting inclusiveness. Inherent in this value was the right of individuals to define their own truth about moral issues like sex. As a result, there were few judgments made about students' individual behavior unless their actions violated the honor code.

PUBLIC VIRTUE

Just as the sample schools integrated private virtues into school life, they also integrated public virtues, such as global understanding, service, and leadership, both locally and abroad. Two schools' English and history curricula centered on their ideals of public virtue; two schools chose a traditional curriculum and used extracurricular time (such as assemblies, advisory, and clubs) to cultivate public virtue; and two others used a hybrid approach. The schools' approach to education for public virtue mirrored their approach to education for private virtue, and as noted earlier, most schools saw private and public virtue as inextricably linked.

Two themes related to public virtue permeated the schools we studied. First, each school ensured that students knew both that what the school provided was exceptional and that the school expected its students to use that gift for a greater good. Second, just as with the culture of honor, there was a clear tension between the schools' achievement culture and their culture of service (though this tension was, again, somewhat lower at East Coast Day School and largely absent at East Coast Boarding School). While the amount of service the school communities provided was staggering, the students often expressed frustration and even cynicism about the schools' motives, seeing the work primarily as résumé-building. The teachers felt some disconnect, too: While many faculty in this study expressed a desire to see their students develop into good people—predominantly defined as people who are generous to those less privileged—not many faculty saw their teaching as a primary means of forming their students' moral direction.

Perhaps most striking, however, was the difference in the magnitude of data we were able to collect on private virtue compared to public virtue. This disparity leads to a simple observation that may be the most powerful one: Schools in the prestigious independent school sector seem to be substantially more committed to the development of private virtue. Or perhaps the explanation is simpler, reinforcing what was noted above: The schools believe that for their population of students, focusing on private virtue will ultimately lead to the good of the whole community. As a veteran teacher at Southern Boys School expressed it, "What comes out on the other end of all of this...I have to believe it is beneficial to society.... We have given them so much here."

There were important differences among the schools' ideals of public virtue, however. At East Coast Boarding School and to a lesser degree Midwestern Day School, promoting justice and equality—especially the rights of minority groups—was the highest ideal. At Southern Boys School, East Coast Day School, and Southern Girls School, the perspective seemed smaller. The latter schools promoted community service and in some cases required it, but the perspective on service did not seem to be well integrated into the program or transformational for the student body.

Midwestern Boarding School, on the other hand, expressly promoted leadership as the highest public virtue. The faculty and administration were resolute in the belief that effective and ethical leadership is critical to healthy communities, and this ideal was well integrated into the fabric of the school. As a result, the students seemed to understand their responsibility to lead; nevertheless, we did not see among the students a belief that leadership was for the greater good.

The degree to which students expressed a genuine belief in their school's ideals of public virtue seemed related, as with the private virtue of honor, to the emphasis placed on such standard markers of academic achievement as college acceptance rates and college admission test scores. The more the schools promoted these traditional markers—as Southern Boys School, Southern Girls School, Midwestern Boarding School, and East Coast Day School did—the less frequently we observed students demonstrating a genuine belief in the ideals of public virtue.

In contrast, students educated in the less traditional schools—East Coast Boarding School and to a substantially lesser degree Midwestern Day School—seemed to think more globally and have more outwardly focused aims. This result may have less to do with the schools' programs than with self-selection, however; the independent school market hinges on the ability of families to choose a school based upon a philosophy, curriculum, and culture consistent with their own view of life. While we sometimes observed conflict between home and school, there was generally a strong connection between what the school promoted, the parents valued, and the students understood.

We did witness one other conflict between private and public virtue: Several of the schools—Southern Girls School, Midwestern Day School, and East Coast Boarding School—attempted to create a neutral moral zone around certain ideas in the name of inclusivity. This effort created some conflict between honoring one's personal beliefs and tolerance toward others. Still, this tension was offset somewhat by the schools' associated moral logic that a student acting with honor will implicitly respect diversity.

ENDNOTES

1 Arthur G. Powell, *Lessons from Privilege: The American Prep School Tradition* (Cambridge, MA: Harvard University Press, 1996).

2 Amy Gutmann, *Democratic Education,* rev. ed. (Princeton, NJ: Princeton University Press, 1999).

3 Patrick J. Wolf, "Civics Exam: Schools of Choice Boost Civic Values," *Education Next* 7, no. 3 (Summer 2007): 66–72.

4 David E. Campbell, "Civic Education in Traditional Public, Charter, and Private Schools: Moving from Comparison to Explanation" in *Making Civics Count: Citizenship for a New Generation,* ed. David E. Campbell, Meira Levinson, and Frederick M. Hess, (Cambridge, MA: Harvard University Press, 2012), 241–44.

3

The Moral Ecology of Formation: Conclusions and Parting Questions

BY JAMES DAVISON HUNTER &
RYAN S. OLSON

The basic premises of this inquiry were demonstrated beyond doubt in our 2018 book: 1) that the environments that children grow up in and, thus, the variety of moral influences that shape them, are astonishingly diverse and 2) that these environments have enormous bearing on how children develop morally. They constitute a complex moral ecology within which children are located and are formed. The picture of children developing outside of history and community as implicitly portrayed in the dominant paradigms of educational and developmental psychology, then, is simply inadequate to a rich understanding of the moral lives of children.

Context matters and it matters decisively. This would seem to be obvious: Every parent, every teacher, every principal and coach, every scout leader, and every youth minister knows this intuitively, for they see the effects of these ecosystems every day and contend with their influence, even as they understand their own presence to be an important, life-shaping dynamic within that environment.

All of this comports with our understanding of character. As we have argued, the form of character is universal—it is constituted by moral discipline, moral attachment, and moral autonomy; the capacities of an individual to inhibit his or her personal appetites or interests on behalf of a greater good, to affirm and live by the ideals of a greater good, and to freely make ethical decisions for or against those goods.[1] Yet because we live in a world of moral diversity, the substance of character is variable. In children, that substance—the content of their character—will never fully mirror the moral ideals of the communities in which they live, though those ideals will have a longstanding influence.

It is essential, then, for scholarship to recognize the significance of these contexts in their variety, to begin to apprehend their complex moral influences, and to understand the complicated way these influences interact with the subjective and intersubjective development of children to shape the content of their character. From here, it is essential to distill this research into strategies of pedagogy that have greater traction with children, their parents and teachers, and the communities they form. Those of us who watch over and care for the young must be attentive to the diversity of contexts that shape them. If we are not attentive to and understanding of these contexts, we are not caring for real, live human beings, but rather abstractions that actually don't exist at all. We can only actually care for the young—and in fact, all people—in their particularity.

The research presented here and in our 2018 book constitutes an initial effort to move decisively in this direction; to provide a richer and more intricate account of the factors involved in the moral and character formation of children. This research begs to be unpacked further, but even at this stage, preliminary observations can be made and questions can be posed for further study.

MORAL ECOLOGY

In every culture—thus, in every moral ecology—there are formal and informal dynamics at work, and these are both very significant. But for the time being, just consider the formal dynamics. Perhaps the most obvious way in which moral ecosystems vary is in the *moral languages* used within those ecosystems. The power of language is the power to name things. By naming the world around us, we define reality, including moral reality. Among other things, language gives us the capacity to name what is right and wrong, good and bad, appropriate and inappropriate; what matters and what doesn't matter; who is a hero and who is a villain; and so on. Needless to say, we make these kinds of evaluations through our naming of the world all of the time. We do this in conversation with others or by ourselves—but even when we are alone, we are never making these evaluations without the social norms of a group or groups in mind. Language, then, provides the joists and beams by which the framework of moral understanding is built.

Human Flourishing and Character

The moral languages we see in this chapter—and especially in our 2018 book that includes the other types of schools are obviously significantly different *across* sectors—the urban public, rural public, charter public, Jewish, Muslim, Catholic, evangelical Protestant, and home-school sectors most clearly. They vary within sectors and even within schools as well. These moral languages can represent long and highly developed traditions of ethical reasoning or more pragmatic, present-oriented idioms. But even in their diversity, consider how much work they do: Among other things, they define the substance of character itself and of personal and public virtue more broadly, and they define different ends or ideals toward which moral action is directed (that is, its ideals of human flourishing).

On a very practical level, if there was a common thread that could be traced through nearly all of the schools, it was a concern with academic achievement on the one hand and service to others on the other hand.* Both of these concerns were infused with moral significance. Where the schools differed was in the relative emphasis the schools placed on them and, more importantly, in the moral grammar used to talk about them. Clustering around

---

* The exceptions were the "unschooling" segment of the homeschooling families, the charter public schools, and the urban district schools. In the urban district schools, service was identified as important for teachers, but not for students.

these anchoring commitments were other moral ideals, some shared in common across the various school sectors, some not. But here again it was in the differences in moral language where the variations became especially distinct.

In the urban district schools, for example, Guhin found that character could mean either "materialist self-advancement" or self-actualization—a need to "be your best self"—or, perhaps, both at the same time. Overall, the moral ideal was for students to "be their best self." Academically, this meant hard work and "grit." As Guhin observed, though, "These values were often divorced from broader questions of what that grit or self-actualization ought to be directed toward." Less prominent in these schools, but still demonstrated by teachers, was an ethics of compassion. Though not often articulated, its importance was generally modeled by teachers in their service to others.

These moral lessons were reflected in all of the charter schools where self-actualization, independence, and high academic performance were also reinforced. Here the mission of the school and the intentionality by which that mission was pursued created a distinct ethos. Thus, the "equity" charter schools focused on developing qualities such as "grit, resilience, excellence, and integrity" *so that* academic success would empower the student to address injustice, either directly through their chosen profession or indirectly by earning an income that would reduce socioeconomic inequality. In the classically oriented school, the ancient intellectual virtues, such as seeking truth, beauty, and well-roundedness, were formally cultivated. In still others, the concern with virtuous behavior was oriented toward the aim of living in harmony with others.

In the rural public schools, Fournier found that it was the pride of particular communities that shaped the moral ethos of schools most comprehensively: Character in these places involved strong links to the local community and thus the obligation to represent one's community well. This was typically framed as "doing the right thing"—an imperative rarely explicated, but assumed to be tacitly understood by students to mean hard work, personal responsibility, resilience, care for others, serving one's community and country, being respectful of elders and the community, and selflessness, especially for the benefit of one's family community, country, and religious congregation.

In several of the *non*public schools, the formal frameworks of moral understanding were starkly different. For example, the evangelical Protestant schools, Sikkink observed, inculcated the message that *all* of a student's life, including academic and worldly success, was ultimately a reflection of the student's ability to achieve a single virtue: "a willingness to place their faith in Jesus Christ and out of gratitude [to God], rather than legalism, to show love to others as God had done to them." God, mediated through scripture, was foundational to all ethics. In this way, a student's character was manifest in a "passion for God" and "Christlikeness," understood "as sacrifice of personal interest for the good of others," not least the "weak" or the social "outcast." Thus, the focus of character among evangelicals was not so much on outward behavior, but on "heart change." In principle, all worldly aspiration and conduct was mediated by the dispositions of the heart in loving obedience to God. It followed that humility was often important to this orientation, insofar as, in Sikkink's words, "the virtuous person in small and unrecognized ways looked out for the hurting or sacrificed their time to help others, especially those who were not easy to help."

The faith-based approach to character and human flourishing emphasized in the evangelical schools was particularly explicit in two of the Catholic schools in this study, though, of course, in a distinctly Catholic, rather than Protestant, way. With the other six Catholic schools, the focus was less on strict adherence to Catholic belief and practice, and more on providing a model of the "good life," enriching the spirituality of students who were Catholic, and following what MacGregor, drawing on Nancy Ammerman,[2] characterized as Golden Rule Christianity— treating others as oneself. Students were expected to be aware and respectful of the church's positions on ethical questions, but students and teachers were not necessarily in line with Catholic teaching on sex and marriage, and teachers encouraged a general tolerance toward different opinions on these matters through open classroom discussion. Here too, in keeping with Catholic tradition, service to one's community, and especially service to the disadvantaged, featured prominently in school life.

The Jewish schools emphasized that a flourishing life meant living up to one's abilities, aiming to be a decent person (*menschlichkeit*), and working to repair the world (*Tikkun Olam*).

In several of the Jewish schools, flourishing was similar to the conservative Catholic and evangelical schools, as it involved offering one's life in service to God, though in this case through the building of a "Jewish character," as one Haredi school head said. Wertheimer found that "Jewish character" involved being careful how one speaks about others and a modesty of behavior and dress that would be conducive to sexual abstinence until marriage. The schools recognized that some character requirements were specific to Jews, while others were universal and demanded of all people equally. In the four Orthodox schools, the moral decisions involved asking, "What does God expect from us, and how will God respond if we disobey?" "Social justice," a commonly occurring theme in discussions of ethics in schools and universities, was emphasized by both ends of the Jewish-sector spectrum—the Haredi 1 and the Community School—but situated within the Jewish tradition.

Across the Islamic school sector, a flourishing life included a strong emphasis on attaining a successful career in the US through hard work and achievement, Glenn found. Yet importantly, this aspiration to assimilate into American culture involved a world picture in which students reinforced their Muslim identity and infused Islamic ideals and practices into all parts of their lives. Islamic faith and tradition, then, were the touchstone of character in these schools, though the national customs of many of the families' countries of origin could also be fused into the schools' ethical ideals. This importation of cultural norms often involved rules that separated boys and girls and regulated their interactions.

In the prestigious independent schools, Wiens found that a life of personal honor or integrity was central to the formal definition of character. Signing an honor code was a practice that reinforced this ideal.* As important was the message of responsibility, born of the privileges the students had received, to contribute to society, especially to the less fortunate. The responsibility to "help others and address systemic poverty and injustice" was commonly heard and given more than lip service. So too were the values of diversity and inclusion. In short, the

---

* Though Wiens's summary in this book mentions signing honor codes only once, her internal research report indicated that several schools in the sample required students to sign an honor code.

codes of *noblesse oblige* were not dead in these schools. More informally, though, the primary concern orienting students' lives in most of the schools was getting into elite colleges or universities; achievement in these realms was seen as integral to having a good life. Character, then, was also defined by the ability to withstand "intense pressures" to excel academically. Under these circumstances, honor and achievement were often at odds, fragmenting the moral messaging in all but one of the schools.

In most of the schools based on alternative pedagogies, there was a fairly distinct understanding of human flourishing, particularly in the three private schools. In the Montessori school, for example, flourishing was defined as a personal sense of peace, the ability to be silent, and to be respectful of other people and the natural world. In the Friends school, flourishing was formally tied to a sense of equality, respecting others' views, and addressing social injustice. Flourishing in the Waldorf school involved the development of the whole student—"spirit, soul, and body." In these three schools, character was viewed as the capacity for respect and empathy, often as evidenced by the ability to function in democratic, community-oriented, egalitarian school cultures. All of these schools emphasized responsibility, self-awareness, a disposition to service, and a desire for social justice through an active engagement with important social issues, an ethic that was reinforced through local service projects oriented toward the needs of the local community. In all, the schools' cultures could have been summed up by an imperative Sikkink heard often, particularly in the Democratic school, to "leave everything better than you found it"—an imperative that could include oneself.

Finally, in the homeschooling sector, ideas about flourishing were "high pluralistic and even flexible," but the two Dill saw most frequently were the "expressivist" and "theistic," corresponding roughly to the nonreligious and religious home-schoolers respectively. Both groups believed their controlled home environments could offer better character formation for their children than traditional schoolrooms would, and they often balanced the relative seclusion of their home environments with activities in the larger home-school community or other civic groups and with an emphasis on such public virtues as tolerance, empathy, and volunteer service. Where they typically differed was in their moral logic. For the nonreligious, the fulfilling life entailed emotional and psychological satisfaction, with children's appreciation for this "blossoming of the inner nature" leading them to care for others' needs. For the religious, flourishing came from living in accordance with God's will as mediated by sacred scripture, with children's understanding of this tradition leading them to develop such classical Christian virtues as prudence and temperance.

Underwriting these various frameworks of moral under-standing were different sources of moral authority that provided the standards for ethical action. This is hardly abstract philoso-phy. Everyone, at one point or another, asks, Why should one be good? Why should one strive to be one's best? Why should one care for another in need? Why should one show respect?

In a pluralistic world, the answers to these questions are var-ied. In our sample schools, the most religiously orthodox school communities looked to the authority of God, whether mediated through scriptures, traditions, or broader communities of faith. Within the urban public schools, the ethos was predominantly a secular therapeutic one, where the individual self, mediated either by one's feelings or one's interests, provided the answers, though even here the reality was opaque in part because the source of moral authority was never openly explored. Within the schools based on alternative pedagogies, moral authority tended to be grounded in distinct and unique conceptions of the indi-vidual, the common good, and one's obligations to serve that good. In none of these settings was moral authority hived off as a single, monolithic reality. In all of these sectors, there was a blending of different sources of authority.

Tension and Conformity

There is a fundamental principle about the formation of iden-tity: Who we are is, in part, a function of who we are not. As individuals and groups, we define ourselves *against* something else. What is distinctive about a moral culture, then, is in part brought into relief by how those who hold it relate to the larger world around them—a world represented through the lens of powerful institutions, such as the entertainment media, social media, political culture and so on.

There is a predictable range: Schools whose mission and moral cultures are in tension with the outside world are conscious of it; other schools that find themselves in complete sympathy with the larger culture see no tension at all. In between, one can find schools operating within a range of ambivalence. Where there is tension, it is reinforced by the conscious effort to differentiate their identities and mission over against something else. What this means is that the points of distinction and of tension are part and parcel of the moral culture of the school and the formation the young experience.

As we might expect, the traditional urban public schools demonstrated a "wariness—from both teachers and students—to say that any kind of life is necessarily better than any other (so long as that life is not causing harm)," which means that there was a sense in which they didn't make much effort to differentiate themselves culturally, missionally, or morally. In some individual cases, though, Guhin observed "heroic" teachers who endeavored "to show compassion to their students and to model such a compassionate life as a meaningful way to live"—something counter to the "code of the street" or to what some students learned at home. Nevertheless, the informal creed of therapeutic self-actualization is part of the curriculum and culture in these schools, and this exists alongside a commitment to individual achievement. Though the focus on "outcomes" is a relatively recent addition to the culture of American public education, the emphasis on test performance as a gateway to the right transcript, grade-point average, and college admissions comports quite well with, and, in fact, reinforces, both therapeutic and meritocratic individualism. Even though the teachers and school staff modeled both compassion and service in their dedication to the students, these virtues were typically expressed as valuable for the students only within a framework of self-actualization or self-advancement.

Rural public schools were typically seen as the hub of their communities and so were well integrated into the surrounding district. They were "an important facilitator of cultural and social cohesion, providing a physical location for social and cultural functions, and producing communal identity," Fournier observed. Thus, they reflected the values of the community— particularly hard work, personal responsibility, pride, patriotism, compassion, respect for others, involvement in one's religious congregation, and honoring military service. The schools actively and informally cultivated a sense of belonging and of being an extended family. If there was a point of tension, it was experienced by parents who were not as involved in the "school community as an extended family" because they were not among those parents who considered their children to be high-achieving in academics or athletics. Those parents tended to be less involved, Fournier suggested, because their own students were not benefiting directly from the schools. Fournier also observed that teachers sought to accustom students to the effects of globalization and to the presence of foreign cultures. To the extent the teachers succeeded, they may have generated some tension between students and the surrounding community, where globalization was less appreciated. For example, Fournier found that immigration was "addressed in some classes…, whether Syrian refugees or Hispanic or Brazilian immigrants. Students and parents were often unaccustomed to seeing large numbers of immigrants in their community, sometimes leaving them with narrow views and, as some teachers noted, little understanding of the larger context. Some teachers worked hard to 'humanize' the experience of immigrants by telling stories of immigrants from their own communities."

The public charter high schools were different inasmuch as they defined themselves as unique missionally, a distinctive reinforced by their families' *choosing* to attend the schools. Here we found schools making a conscious effort to distinguish themselves and their culture from the surrounding world— from home life, in the case of the "equity" schools, and from other kinds of schools, particularly the traditional public schools. In the "equity" schools, educators especially focused on "overcoming racial inequalities" by preparing their low-income, minority students with meritocratic, middle-class values. Other charter schools differentiated themselves by the moral sources they invoked—in one case, the Greco-Roman classics, and in another case, Eastern philosophy—both of which could conflict with popular culture and require countercultural attitudes and behavior.

In the same way, it was the distinctive identity and philosophical mission of the alternative-pedagogy schools that set them apart from both popular culture and traditional public education. Whatever the school staffs' explicit articulation of these ideas, the schools seemed most clearly distinguished from the mainstream by their practices and the staffs' modeling of desirable—frequently egalitarian—behaviors. Most of these schools critiqued cultural norms of "celebrity, consumption, and sexuality." They also limited the use of technology in classrooms and, in at least one case, these limitations were based on educational theory and the school's founding documents.

The prestigious independent schools were conscious of their privilege and higher academic standards compared to other schools; they also pursued the moral responsibilities that they felt came with those advantages. Despite their differences from other schools, they conformed to some key cultural norms of many of the public schools. Several of the schools worked to create a "neutral moral zone around certain ideas in the name of inclusivity," Wiens wrote. She also found that the schools largely granted students the ability to "define their own truth" as part of that ethos of supposed neutrality, and that "there were few judgments made about individual behavior" (at least outside a school's honor code).

As one would expect, the religious schools were, by definition, distinctive, though not uniformly so. Within the evangelical Protestant schools, there was a sense that popular culture was not friendly toward Christian faith. Their wariness was oriented not only toward the "relativism and hedonism" of popular culture, but also toward education credentials, an exclusive focus on career success, and on politics. All of these schools made some effort to prepare students to resist these cultural realities. Perhaps surprisingly, the evangelical schools did not politicize their distrust toward the world. Rather the overall concern was "how to live faithfully." One manifestation of this emphasis was in the ways these schools generally downplayed worldly success in favor of the serving professions.

The Catholic schools in our sample were also less combative than one might imagine. For example, though the Catholic Church is known for its conservative positions on sexual ethics, in most of the schools, teachers encouraged respectful debate on such issues. It was "hard to imagine any of the teachers we interviewed describing homosexuality as a sin," MacGregor observed—though faculty at one of the schools "would likely have said engaging in homosexual *sex* was sinful in the same way that any extramarital sex would be sinful." Rather, the schools generally saw themselves as pedagogically and educationally superior to the local public schools. In one case, a school "promoted itself as more authentically Catholic than other Catholic schools."

The larger puzzle of Jewish identity is deeply historic and it has long played out in their schools. There has always been a tension between what the school taught and what students have "absorbed from the wider culture." Not surprisingly, then, the Jewish schools both differentiated themselves from, and identified with, the broader culture to varying degrees. The Orthodox schools warned students that poor behavior in public could lead people to "cast aspersions on all Jews and even on Judaism itself" and "risked besmirching God's name." Promoting Jewish identity, though, meant different things. In the Haredi girls school, it was understood that to be a Jew required taking countercultural positions. In the Community school, there was a distinctively "Jewish religious approach to misbehavior," though a course in Jewish ethics invoked progressive ideology even as it appropriated Jewish texts. In the centrist Orthodox school, the student-developed school code of conduct did not stand out as Jewish and didn't use Hebrew terms or Jewish concepts; the same could be said of the rationale for its strict dress code. In general, Jewish schools in the study were willing to "adapt curricula and programs developed in broader American educational circles" on such topics as bullying, sexuality, and substance abuse, while the public schools' recent emphases on "grit" and "empowerment" had entered the Jewish schools too. The effect of the schools' character education, at least in non-Haredi schools, was to make Jewish students "equally open to connection with non-Jews,...attentive to the plight of non-Jewish minorities, and aware of developments in Jewish life and American society at large," Wertheimer observed. Even though students and faculty seemed to be aware of the "clash of worldviews" between Jewish and non-Jewish worlds, a therapeutic framework grounded in learner-centered and developmental psychological approaches was prevalent, except in parts of the Haredi subsector.

This ambivalence was present within the Islamic schools as well. On the one hand, it was widely recognized that American culture would pose challenges to living as a devout Muslim. At the same time, teachers and administrators in these schools seemed eager to help students to assimilate into American culture. Glenn found that the solution to this tension was to impart the "underlying principles"—not just the rules—of the Islamic faith so that students would be able to navigate the challenges in unfamiliar situations. Students also experienced tensions between the identity and mores of their family's country of origin and American culture. Here the solution was thought to be the cultivation and practice of a "pure" version of Islam that transcended nationality.

The very premise of homeschooling is a distrust of mainstream culture and its educational establishment. Dill found that the "moral coherence of the family" was typically pitted against "the larger incoherence of the world outside of the family." This was true not only for religious families, but for nonreligious families as well. This did not mean a rejection of the world *tout court*, but rather a disposition to relate to the world—and its educational offerings—on the family's own terms. Reaching outside the home often meant looking for and associating with other families who viewed the world in a similar way.

ENDOWMENTS, THICK AND THIN

The various "moral philosophies" that distinguish these schools is only the most obvious way in which their moral ecologies of differ. Another way they vary is found in the kinds of *moral endowments* they offer in the task of formation. The moral endowments or resources found within different schools tend to range between "thick" and "thin," and they can even vary within school sectors. For Michael Walzer, to whom we owe this distinction, the concept of "thin" morality tends to refer to idioms that we can generally all agree on. They often find expression in ostensible universals or abstract procedures for which there are few if any disagreements.[3] And though typically found in simplistic expressions or symbols, thin moral reasoning is often the place of cross-cultural agreement. By contrast, "thick" moral reasoning and discourse is not abstract, but concrete; bounded by the history, tradition, and the practices of lived experience in particular communities.

Sources

Moral thickness and thinness take form in several dimensions. One of these dimensions concerns the actual sources that elucidate the frameworks of moral understanding. There are ways in which these were obvious in our schools, but empirically, they were not uniformly so.

The most prominent examples of "thickness" in this regard came from the religious schools, which drew upon sacred texts, traditions, and exemplars as their sources of moral authority and imagination. For the evangelical Protestant schools and religious homeschoolers, the good was rooted in the life and example of Jesus Christ as mediated through scripture and personal experience. Common language coming from the bible provided authority for school policies, as well as "boundaries to any conversation or debate about a school's practices within the school community," as Sikkink put it. Many of these schools also draw upon the classical tradition of education.

Similarly, the Catholic high schools drew from a "common repertoire of Catholic resources" for religious education and gave prominence to narratives about school founders and patron saints, and the like. These sources of moral authority were also reflected in the symbols (such as crucifixes) found throughout the school environments. Likewise, Wertheimer found that "every type of Jewish school grounded its character education in traditional Jewish sources, regardless of how untraditional its outlook." He observed, for instance, a Conservative high school orientation retreat that helped prepare the students for the Jewish Day of Atonement with texts like "excerpts from the liturgy of the high holidays, prophetic readings on Yom Kippur, [and] the writings of Maimonides, Abraham Joshua Heschel, [and] contemporary Jewish thinkers." In Orthodox schools, Jewish ethical and legal texts concerning responsibilities toward others were taught. At the Community High School, biblical and rabbinic texts also informed enforcement of behavioral expectations, including the use of rabbinic notions of repentance to deal with misbehaviors. Justification for certain pedagogies was also drawn from rabbinic texts. In the Islamic high schools, there was a constant reference to Islamic religious texts and practices, including the traditions of Islamic jurisprudence. From their expertise in these texts and traditions, school staff derived an authority to help to contextualize Islamic faith and identity for their students.

Perhaps less historically deep, but nevertheless rich in sources were the alternative-pedagogy schools, whose moral authority was rooted in the educational philosophies and programs of their founders in most cases. This turn was especially prominent in the Montessori and Waldorf schools, where the writings of Maria Montessori and Rudolf Steiner, respectively, were guides. The Democratic school had a theoretical lineage traced to the American countercultural movements of the 1960s; the Friends school consciously appropriated the Quaker ethical tradition; and the New Tech school drew on a coherent project-based-learning methodology. These sources had formative effects that worked together with articulated messages about private and public virtue.

In the same way, the "virtue" charter school and the "relational" charter school drew from the sources of Greco-Roman virtue ethics and Eastern philosophy, respectively, which provided sources of educational consistency and motive for the school community.

The rural schools in this study did not explicitly identify moral sources, but did practice a practical, on-the-ground communitarianism in which authority was drawn from local traditions and relationships. This was similar to the prestigious independent schools, which were deeply conscious of their own community traditions and legacy and the honor and pride that went with it. While these could pale in comparison to the pressures of academic achievement, they were, nevertheless, a vital part of the backdrop of moral expectation in the school culture.

In the urban public schools, there were pervasive commitments to moral inclusivity and within that framework, to self-actualization and to "grit," mostly meaning perseverance and a work ethic. While woven into the policies of the school, the symbolic and textual sources for framing discussions of these ethical qualities were not extensive.

Articulation, Formal (Through Instruction)...

A second and related way in which the moral ecologies vary in relative thickness or thinness is the degree to which a moral culture is articulated, whether formally in the classroom or informally in the relationships between teachers and students.

The presence of texts, traditions, and exemplars as sources for framing the moral culture of the school certainly create conditions conducive for explanation and illumination, but their presence did not mean that they are always drawn upon. Here, there was remarkable variation across school sectors and within them.

As a rule, we tended to see greater articulation in the private and religious schools than in the public schools.*

In the evangelical Protestant schools, Sikkink found that teachers not only taught the biblical text itself, but also sought to "engage students with the ethical issues of their generation and other practical questions regarding how to live faithfully in relation to others and the surrounding culture." That surrounding culture was not engaged by the schools in terms of "societal injustice and activist engagement"—except by the Mennonite school—but Sikkink did observe that by teaching the students to serve others, the schools built in them the "trust, sacrifice, [and] reciprocity… that serve as a foundation for civic involvements." Across the curriculum, teachers intentionally incorporated religious and spiritual elements in class, including discussions of controversial topics. Catholic schools, similarly, had religious instruction as a part of the school curriculum and presented school founders and patron saints as moral models. Like the evangelical schools, Catholic schools didn't shy away from "constructive dialogue about sensitive issues" in the classroom. Interestingly, discussion of various moral lessons was common in the Catholic schools' literature classes. MacGregor also found that political engagement was not "a robust emphasis" and that the formation of public virtue through civic instruction was perfunctory in a senior-level course, though the schools' civics electives were more engaging.

Moral discourse in the Jewish schools was generally also thick, though some schools used theological language more than others. The curriculum often included explicit teaching of what a life in service to God involved. Teachers would extend these principles to a range of concrete behavior, such as premarital sex and combatting social injustices. Jewish moral teaching even informed such nitty-gritty issues as gossip, cheating, slandering others on social

---

* This is not to say that some individual public schools, like the Virtue Charter, did not achieve an articulation that may have rivaled or exceeded that of the religious schools—just that the overall trend appears to have been in the religious schools' favor.

media, and sex. Wertheimer noted that even a school that was less comfortable using theological language appropriated a religious concept to discipline students who broke the rules, requiring *teshuva*—"a rabbinic category of repentance involving both apology and repair." And regarding public virtues, Wertheimer found that with the exception of Haredi schools, "considerable attention" was devoted to civic education, including observation of Veterans Day and other ways of honoring US and Israeli veterans.

In the Islamic schools, moral discourse was also embedded in the religious discourse—sermons, prayers, and the like. The personal virtues were framed most dramatically by the separation of boys and girls in school and through its accompanying Islamic rationales. Glenn noted that when behavioral issues needed tackling, they were addressed by brief talks after daily prayers and by "longer assemblies with formal sermons on Fridays." The public virtues of citizenship were often taught more indirectly, as the subtext of assimilation to, and of service of, the dominant American culture—a culture in which school staff emphasized Muslims were "participating and loyal citizens."

In the prestigious independent schools, part of the curriculum was set aside for teaching ideals of public virtue, though, Wiens observed, "not many faculty saw their teaching as a primary means of forming their students' moral direction." Among homeschooling families, especially those with religious motivations, many explicitly taught such scriptural or classical personal virtues as temperance or prudence, while public virtues were formed by civic education, diverse co-op settings, and robust simulations of legislative experiences.

The alternative-pedagogy schools in our sample tended to teach character and citizenship through experiential learning opportunities such as "town meetings," student government, grade-level meetings with administrators, and practices that fostered mutual commitment to every student's success. Thus, the schools did seek to embed the teaching of virtue in aspects of their cultures, and they expected teachers to find ways of incorporating it into their instruction. Schools also taught it indirectly through an emphasis, for example, on the "whole child," including his or her social nature, or on "social justice in humanities courses, especially regarding issues of racial equality, LGBTQ rights, and gender equality," Sikkink wrote. "Honor councils" were prevalent in half of the schools, and expectations included not violating academic integrity through cheating or plagiarism, whether these were viewed as sins in themselves or symptomatic of underlying difficulties. These episodes of moral instruction were provided by adults and, in the case of honor councils, even by peers.

In rural district schools, explicit teaching of character, citizenship, or values occurred, but the moral ideals—such as commitment to community or industriousness—were frequently articulated in only general terms. Moral reasoning and explaining motivation were less observable. For example, during discussions of controversial ethical topics, teachers attempted to remain neutral and "refrain from providing serious direction on what was right and what was wrong." In the rural schools, moral instruction was founded on one-to-one relationships, especially when students approached a teacher for advice or support. Much the same could be said of the urban public schools, where we again found less detailed specification of the beliefs, values, and rationales the school stood for. This didn't mean that there were no values. To the contrary, those values and ideals were woven into the pedagogy of key teachers or within certain practices honored by the school.

...And Informal (Through "Catching")

The articulation of a moral culture through explicit teaching is important and, needless to say, variable. What these case studies also consistently show is the importance of the *informal* articulation of a moral culture through the example of teachers and other adults in the school community. The moral example of teachers unquestionably complemented the formal instruction students received, but arguably, it was *far* more poignant to, and influential upon, the students themselves. Certainly, this was the impression in the trenches. As one principal of an Islamic school put it, "We want *every* teacher to be a character teacher.... Every class is for the character first then the knowledge. Because knowledge without character is just information." A teacher in one of the alternative-pedagogy schools said, "You can talk all day long. If you don't walk the walk, they're not buying it and they know the difference." And in the evangelical Protestant sector, Sikkink wrote that "one principal explained that the key to influencing student socialization was not 'curriculums, buildings, outward things, but the people we hire. Men and women who align with [our school]. They have to be at the top of their game, with a passion for [our] mission.'"

The premise of the modeling relationship is established from the outset: As a rule, students want their teachers to think well of them and respect them, and they recognize teachers as role models as they do other adults, such as coaches, administrators, and parents.

The importance of modeling the good is especially important in the public schools because explicit moral teaching is (or is perceived to be) fraught with disagreement, controversy, or legal challenges. In the urban schools, for example, teachers often did not have the time or would not make the time to teach moral lessons in their classrooms. One teacher noted the objections he'd heard "from other teachers and from people in the community… that teaching character is much too complicated and it would be too difficult to come to a common set of values." When teachers in this sector did engage in moral discussion, it was more likely that they did it "idiosyncratically" and on their own. At the same time, these teachers were often praised for their compassion. Though the language was not often used, there appeared to be a widely shared sensibility across the sectors that love can make the difference. One rural public school teacher ventured that love was "doing what's best [for and] serving that kid." For this teacher, who spoke for many in Fournier's sample, "if you just have teachers that love the kids, they are going to know what's best to do."

For this reason, identifying and hiring the right teachers— those who are both knowledgeable and skilled as teachers but also models of the virtues the school wanted to instill—was a vital concern in all of the schools.

Practices

The moral and missional ethos of a school was reinforced through a range of practices, or routinized actions—some formal, some informal—all oriented toward giving tangible expressions to the school's values and beliefs. These included school mottoes, honor codes, school assemblies, mission statements, dress codes, statues, stories, student handbooks and contracts outlining behavioral expectations, and the like. Their presence or absence, their use or lack of use, was variable in different schools and school sectors, but they all contributed to the relative thickness or thinness of each school's moral ecology. All of it bears on the likelihood children will "catch" character.

Many of the schools also had the practice of community service built into their education. Though its value was sometimes questioned by students and parents, community service was an important part of the schools' moral ecology and an important way to reinforce the school's ethical mission. Seven of the eight Catholic schools MacGregor studied, for example, had service programs, and three of the eight required student service—usually about 100 hours and involving "direct interaction with people in need." In all of the Jewish schools in our sample, time serving others in the community was also a requirement, ranging between 26 hours per year to three hours per week, with the most being required by Haredi schools. The evangelical Protestant schools "facilitated opportunities for short-term mission trips and other forms of service, offering other important avenues for students' faith and moral formation." Wiens found a "staggering" amount of service being done by students at prestigious independent schools, even though the students often suspected that the primary purpose was to build the students' résumés. Service days and projects were also popular in Islamic schools, and the rural district schools encouraged volunteer work.

And Social Ecology

A final way in which we see the dynamics of thickness and thinness of a moral ecology in play is in the social support surrounding the child. There is considerable evidence that strong social support contributes crucially, if not decisively, to their academic success in school, whether that support comes from parents and family, youth organizations, or religious communities. The thickness of social ties also bears positively on the formation of a stable self-identity and, by extension, a child's moral character.

There is a skeptical view that suggests that tight social networks of oversight provide an ongoing surveillance over the young person, giving them little room to experiment or make mistakes. The more positive construction would be that a close community provides a watchful and loving attentiveness that allows the young person to thrive. Arguably, thick social ties can be both, with the effect of being both empowering and disempowering. There is much more we need to learn about this. What is clear is that empirically, the various school sectors look very different in their social ecology.

Perhaps the most socially integrated school context was the home school. Against some caricatures, our homeschoolers generally didn't withdraw in isolation from the larger world. Most of these families aligned with institutions and groups that shared a degree of the family's moral framework. These might include co-op groups of other homeschooling families, scouting, religious congregations' programs, and volunteer organizations. One homeschooling mother said, "From a moral perspective, I feel like everybody's sending them the same message [in our home-school group].... I feel like yes, I'm their parent, but they have 20 other parents there that are all expecting that they essentially hold the same moral, high standard for themselves, so in that sense I feel like that they're getting reinforced."

There was a similar level of social density or thickness of ties in the rural schools for reasons we've already observed. School personnel were often alumni of the schools, which helped to reinforce connections to the broader local community. Multigenerational relationships were important also. One principal said, "We have grandparents [of current students] that graduated from here.... 'Why, why do you want me to be that?' 'Well, because! Because your grandparents want you to! Because your parents want you to! Because that's how you're successful!'" Fournier found that "everyone at least knows *of* one another's family, their reputation." The students' "sense of belonging" built trust, which increased the authority of school personnel, who would, in these small communities, happen upon their students outside of school in the community, thereby further increasing social bonds and trust. Fournier also found that religious clubs were active in the rural schools, whether a religious organization's staff person was socializing with students in the school or offering an after-school program as a "natural extension" of the community's culture.

The very existence of an educational market in the US highlights the fact that parents have different reasons for sending their children to a school other than the local public school. If they can afford it, or if they win a place through a lottery, the motive can be to take advantage of the school's vibrant learning environment, its competitive academic placement, its healthy moral ethos, its religious instruction, its physical safety. We know from other research that there are often more reasons than one. Yet overall, where there is a choice and where parents also pay tuition, they are likely to be more involved. Whether and how much they are involved is influenced by different reasons.

The evangelical Protestant schools were "active in working with parents toward the students' faith formation," and being from a common evangelical subculture made a school's "active intervention in students' lives more likely." Interestingly, within the private religious schools, the church, parish, synagogue and mosque were not as actively involved or supportive as we had hypothesized. Though religious congregations may be more active elsewhere, in this inquiry, it was primarily the parents that formed the main social support for their kids. To the extent we were able to learn about parental support, parents' involvement varied a lot. Yet parents were in some cases expected to go beyond paying tuition and contribute their time and energy. For example, Sikkink found that in at least one evangelical school, parents were encouraged to "read Scripture with their family during the week" and to take part in parenting seminars—rewarded, in one case, by discounted tuition fees. In the other school sectors, parents were sometimes required to volunteer.

In the prestigious independent schools, the parents and schools formed a reasonably strong partnership: What the school promoted, the parents valued, and the students understood and embraced—at least up to a point, since, Wiens observed, "there was...some disparity between the priority the schools placed on moral formation and the primary reasons parents chose the schools." That is, many of the parents enrolled their children in these schools primarily for the purposes of giving them a quality education and a competitive academic advantage, so there was often a discrepancy between academics and character formation, a tension not lost on the students. Even so, in the effort to instill a code of honor, parents generally gave the schools a fair amount of leeway to enforce school policies regarding students' behavior. There was a similar dynamic (and similar motives) at work in some of the alternative schools—

especially the Friends school and the New Tech school, according to Sikkink's full report—and in the public charter schools. Parents generally were on board with and supportive of the school's mission. The partial exception was the "equity" charter schools, where school personnel sometimes felt they had to overcome counterproductive parental attitudes.

In the urban public schools, parents, guardians, and leaders of other institutions did not appear to be very involved in the schools' formation process; the school was the focal point of formation, though Guhin did observe a school administrator taking care not to openly disagree with what a student was taught at home in front of a student.

In Sum

Context matters. There are massive differences in the moral ecologies of different schools in America today. While no one imagines for a moment that these moral frameworks and their cultural logics are effortlessly and seamlessly transmitted to students, they do comprise "the waters they swim in." Their influence cannot help but be significant for the moral formation of the children in their keeping.

To be sure, hard work and achievement is a common thread throughout American education. In a meritocratic society, this is hardly surprising. How it was understood and reflected in the various ethical languages ranged widely. An achieving self could be one who is responsive to God or who is trying to represent one's religion or one's community or one's family well. Even acknowledging these differences, hard work and achievement are anything but the only thread making up the fabric of moral life in schools.

The moral ecologies that define our 10 sectors of American education represent a complexity that needs to be understood much better than it currently is. But the challenge of sorting out the complex contextual influences goes farther.

In highlighting the differences in the moral ecologies of schools, it is important to repeat that none of these represents hermetically sealed, self-contained ways of thinking or practicing ethical behavior. Jewish schools, for example, differ amongst themselves, as do Catholic, evangelical and Muslim schools. Homeschooling parents also operate in radically different and opposing ways. And no public school is identical to any other.

Moreover, syncretism—or the amalgamation of different streams of thought and practice—abounds in these schools. Programs addressing such problems as bullying, social media, sexuality, substance abuse, and cheating are drawn from public or nonsectarian schools and readily embraced by religious schools. At the same time, many public schools are using "mindfulness" programs, and these are found in the Jewish schools as well,* though Hasidic schools draw on their own contemplative tradition. Secular, personalist moral understanding infuses the religious schools to varying degrees and, in some cases, various religious influences are powerfully present within secular educational settings.

THE CHALLENGE AHEAD

What we have here is the start of a framework for making sense of those differences. Elaborating that framework and understanding its complexity is a task that will continue. But understanding is not enough. It is essential to press further and make this framework usable by those who work with students every day and those who make and enforce educational policies.

The point is debatable, of course, but one could make a reasonable case that in a world as complex and challenging as ours, the ideal moral ecology is one that provides moral resources to children that are *both* thick and thin; thick in ways that provide coherent articulation rooted in practices that are authoritative without being authoritarian, yet balanced by thinner, more universal norms that bind people across traditions and communities.

The problem in late-modern America is in the lack of balance between thick and thin in our moral cultures. On the one hand, the thickness of our moral communities is easily politicized, leaving our democratic system fragmented, polarized, and, well, broken. Yet the thinness of our shared culture—defined more by consumerism and popular culture than anything else—tends to dissolve the genuine ethical thickness of public discourse and the rich thickness of moral communities. What is more, the dominant paradigm of moral and character formation on offer to

---

* The *Mussar* school of thought is increasingly popular, and this draws from philosophical and theological texts originating from nineteenth century Lithuania.

schools and parents tends to reinforce, rather than resist, these tendencies.[4] Yet this is the context in which schools and families find themselves and, in so many words, want to resist.

The moral philosopher Charles Taylor insisted that it is the concrete particularities that lead us to the sources of morality, precisely the ethical substance that motivates and sustains our commitment to benevolence and justice, to goodness and fair play. High ethical standards, he argued, require the strong sources that come from the thick moral traditions. These also provide the foundations for stronger moral selves capable of engaging the complexities and contradictions of the world, the victories and setbacks endemic to everyone's life. As we've seen, the thicker the moral culture of the school, the more coherent it was and the more cohesive an environment it provided for the young. These are the environments within which personal and public virtue is both learned and absorbed; both "taught and caught."

On a promising note, virtually no school in our study overtly politicized their mission and identity. Perhaps, then, education can lead the way. But if it does, we must all better comprehend the complex realities facing our children, understand the educational challenges of forming them well, and reckon with the dangers if we don't.

ENDNOTES

1   See again James Davison Hunter, *The Death of Character: Moral Education in an Age Without Good or Evil* (New York: Basic Books, 2000), 16.

2   Nancy Ammerman, "Golden Rule Christianity: Lived Religion in the American Mainstream," in *Lived Religion in America: Toward a History of Practice*, ed. David D. Hall (Princeton, NJ: Princeton University Press, 1997), 280.

3   Michael Walzer, *Thick and Thin: Moral Argument at Home and Abroad* (Notre Dame, IN: University of Notre Dame Press, 1994).

4   See again James Davison Hunter, *The Death of Character: Moral Education in an Age Without Good or Evil* (New York: Basic Books, 2000).

4

Framework & Resource Overview For Leaders of Schools & Associations

BY RYAN S. OLSON

The Institute for Advanced Studies in Culture (IASC) at the University of Virginia shares more than 30 years of research to benefit the public by serving strategically placed leaders. The research of the Institute's Colloquy on Culture & Formation answers the question, What does it take to form good children, wise leaders, and virtuous citizens? As of 2022, the colloquy is chaired by Prof. Angel Adams Parham. The New Paradigms Lab (NPL) at the Institute translates our research for the benefit of leaders who face the challenges of our late-modern society. The New Paradigm Lab's advisory group in formation consists of educational leaders from the national, state, and local levels, including several heads from independent schools. Membership applications to join the NPL advisory group are considered on a rolling basis and can be found at https://iasculture.org/research/new-paradigms-lab.

The Institute's New Paradigms Lab partners with school leaders and boards around the world to create healthy moral ecologies centered on schools. Using cutting edge research from the Institute and partners, we come alongside school communities based on the Moral Ecology Framework. Schools can evaluate their progress annually against the framework with the Moral Ecology Assessment. To strengthen and transform their own moral ecology to form good character, they can participate in annual training for transformative leadership with monthly cohort support. To deepen the impact on faculty and students, they can adopt aligned character curricula such as the Nyansa Character Curriculum for K–12, as well as sustain daily conversations and awareness of key insights by contributing content and applying peer learning from CultureFeed Educators at culturefeed.com.

These resources are drawn from research conducted by the Institute for more than 20 years. These include James Davison Hunter, *The Death of Character* (2000); J.D. Hunter and Carl Desportes Bowman, *The Politics of Character* (2000); C.D. Bowman, Jeffrey Dill & J.D. Hunter, *Culture of American Families* (2012); Ryan S. Olson, "Character Education," in Oxford Bibliographies Online (2015); J.D. Hunter and R.S. Olson, *The Content of Their Character: Inquiries into the Varieties of Moral Formation* (2018); J.D. Hunter, C.D. Bowman & Kyle Puetz, *The Context of Character: Teen Moral Formation in the 21st Century* (2021), various issues of *The Hedgehog Review*, and multiple journal articles by scholars at the Institute's Survey Lab and Colloquy on Culture & Formation that were prepared with support from the Kern Family Foundation, the John Templeton Foundation, the Donchian Foundation, and major donors.

MORAL ECOLOGY FRAMEWORK v 3.0

The Moral Ecology Framework captures more than two decades of research on character formation by the Institute for Advanced Studies in Culture. The framework is compatible with, complementary to, and enabling of many models and programs for character formation. These include the Jubilee Centre's Framework for Character Education, Center for Curriculum Redesign, the Leader in Me, VIA Institute on Character, the Montessori model, the 11 Principles from Character. Org, University of Chicago Framework for Young Adult Success, Program for Leadership and Character at Wake Forest University, and many others.

Moral Ecology Framework™

Formative Agent

Mode of Agency	Alignment of Character	Context	• Complementing • Overcoming
	Contents of Character	Moral Traditions	• Sourcing
	Transmission of Character	Organization	• Modeling & Embedding • Teaching • Practicing
	Structure of Character	Person	• Instilling Discipline • Nurturing Attachment • Personalizing Autonomy

Practices of Formation

The influences upon a person's character—the **FORMATIVE AGENTS**—are both personal and institutional. Most commonly recognized in educational research and practice is reflexive agency, or a person shaping his or her own moral knowledge, habits, attitudes, and motivations. Such formation is achieved by recognizing the structure or form of character.

Thus, character has a common structure or form based on human nature that is universal, regardless of historical period, tradition, community, religion, race, nationality, and the like. The **STRUCTURE OF CHARACTER** consists of moral discipline, moral attachment, and moral autonomy. This form is recognized and shaped **in individuals** when a person...

- **Instills discipline** by fostering the personal capacity to resist temptation or deviations from the good one is pursuing,

- **Nurtures attachment** by inculcating the personal, emotional, moral, and/or spiritual connection to a confession and/or cause greater than oneself within a moral community, and

- **Personalizes autonomy** by taking responsibility for one's thoughts, attitudes, beliefs, actions, habits, and behaviors.

An ORGANIZATION—such as a school, charter school network, or school district—forms a person's character through explicit and implicit means to transmit character to the person with the practices of modeling and embedding, teaching, and providing opportunities for practicing.

Thus, the **transmission of character** refers to the various means by which character is learned and put into practice, namely...

- **Modeling and embedding** by exhibiting character in the personnel, rituals, and built environment,

- **Teaching** by articulating lessons and insights from the moral sources, and

- **Practicing** by habituating the moral content and practices intentionally and routinely.

This is where various compatible character curricula and programs, such as those named above, would fit, potentially shaping all three practices for the transmission of character, depending on how thorough the implementation is.

The organization is nested within a **MORAL TRADITION** or **MORAL TRADITIONS**, whether recognized and explicitly taught, or tacit and inarticulately formative. Moral traditions form through their contents, which, when effective, are explicitly sourced in practice.

Thus, the **contents of character** refers to the moral and ethical substance of character. These are the animating faiths or philosophies that provide a "picture" of the good life to which one holds and at which one's life is aimed, as well as the sources that provide the motivation for moral action. The key practice for the contents of character is...

- **Sourcing** by strengthening "roots" in the texts, traditions, and/or exemplars from religious, philosophical, pedagogical, and/or national origins that are authoritative in the school community.

Finally, the person, the organization, and the moral tradition exist within a **CONTEXT** that is historical, cultural, and institutional.

The **alignment of character** involves the ecosystem of institutions that rest upon distinctive ideals, beliefs, obligations, prohibitions, and commitments rooted in and reinforced by well-established social practices. The institutions within the ecosystem include the family, school, peers, youth organizations, social media, religious congregations, athletic leagues, and so on. The practices that are essential to the alignment of character are...

- **Complementing** by identifying and working in concert with the elements of the moral ecology that are in agreement with the moral tradition, and

- **Overcoming** by identifying and subverting or mitigating the influence of elements of the moral ecology that are not aligned with the moral tradition.

TRAINING & CONSULTATIONS FOR TRANSFORMATIVE LEADERSHIP

Based on the most sophisticated social theory and historical research our scholars have found, the agent at the core Institute's theory of change is a **network of leaders united in common cause for human flourishing in thriving communities.** Transformational leaders expertly guide change. Based on this change management model, we train leaders—especially leaders of leaders—and nurture networks to leverage their spheres of influence for the common good. Networked with other like-minded leaders, the leaders we serve discover and strengthen the intellectual resources, moral courage, visionary imagination, and lessons of experienced practice from their peers.

We also provide a larger framework to analyze and enhance the contribution of schools to their local communities using the Thriving Communities Framework. This framework consists of six civic endowments. Three of the endowments are classical: The Good, The True, and The Beautiful; three of the endowments are modern: The Prosperous, The Just & Well-Ordered, and The Sustainable. This framework has been adopted by several U.S. cities and by the Organisation of Economic Co-operation and Development (OECD).

Training sessions in these frameworks and materials range from one to four days, depending on the depth of a school or association's interest and commitment. Follow-up consultations are offered and structured based on the needs and goals of a school or association's leadership team. To support ongoing training and development, CultureFeed Education (http://www. culturefeed.com) offers curated, peer-generated content that can be used by faculty, staff, parents, and other stakeholders.

MORAL ECOLOGY ASSESSMENT

With the Moral Ecology Assessment, members of a school and community evaluate their effectiveness based on the nine practices of a healthy moral ecology outlined above. Detailed Moral Ecology Assessment reports identify areas of strength and improvement. To be considered for adoption of the Moral Ecology Assessment, submit an application at https://iasculture.org/ research/new-paradigms-lab.

CHARACTER CURRICULUM

Recognizing the diverse communities that are educating young people, we support a variety of approaches to teaching and modeling character. This variety exists across ten broad sectors of schools: public urban, public rural/suburban, public charter, independent, home schools, Jewish, Islamic, Catholic, Evangelical, and pedagogical schools such as Montessori, military academies, and STEM schools. Requests to evaluate a curriculum's alignment with the Moral Ecology Model can be made at https:// iasculture.org/research/new-paradigms-lab.

The first full curriculum we offer is the Nyansa Classical Character Curriculum. The program draws on three distinctive moral sources: classical mythology, the Black intellectual tradition, and (where appropriate, in private schools) the Christian tradition. The curriculum is available for grades 9-12. The curriculum can be adopted and adapted in many ways including embedding in existing curricula and instruction, after school programs, lessons during the instructional day, summer programs, youth athletics, and the like. To learn more, visit https://iasculture.org/research/ new-paradigms-lab.